The
APOSTOLIC
DIGEST

ABRIDGED EDITION

Compiled from Sources which
have borne the Imprimatur

Michael Malone
Editor

CATHOLIC TREASURES
MONROVIA, CALIFORNIA

Whosoever among you fear God, it is to you the word of this salvation is sent.

Acts of the Apostles 13:26

CONTENTS

Book IV
THE BOOK OF CHRISTIANS

Book V
THE BOOK OF OBEDIENCE

Book VI
THE BOOK OF SENTIMENTAL EXCUSES

Book VII
THE BOOK OF IGNORANT NATIVES

FOREWORD

This little endeavor to catalogue the traditional stand of Holy Mother the Church is as complete as it will ever need to be. The Catholic Faith has been delivered to us once and for all times as a glorious "deposit," St. Paul assures us (I Tim. 6:20), and thus all we have to do is hold onto it for ourselves, offer it wholesale to our neighbors, and pass it along intact to our children. The unfortunate fact that so many of our modern clergy appear to lag behind is no excuse whatever for the rest of the Catholic faithful to neglect our own responsibilities.

Someone might object that I may seem to have been overly selective in the gathering and collating of my quotations. Perhaps. But, whenever a warrior goes into battle, he chooses only the most powerful of his weapons. Therefore, permit me to make for my own the words in which the Angelic Doctor, St. Thomas Aquinas, introduces his own *Golden Chain* of Scriptural commentaries:

> In quoting the testimonies of so many Saints, it was necessary many times to cut away some parts so as to avoid undue length; and, for greater clarity, I have omitted words and, according to my purpose, rearranged the actual sequence of parts quoted.

Moreover, in order to achieve the brevity required in abridgments, this version will, unlike our Complete Edition, present citations without the customary ellipses which signify the omission of unnecessary text. To further facilitate a greater fluency in reading, the authors and their sources are sequentially indexed at the conclusion of the work.

It is true that, in a compilation such as this, there will always exist the danger that the editor may misunderstand (and thus misrepresent) the intent of the author in selecting any given quotation from his writings. However, it is impossible to misunderstand the meaning of the Church in the clarity of her infallible definitions, for they constitute the solitary interpretation of dogma which is allowed us as followers of Jesus Christ. Therefore, it has not been my endeavor to present the mind of individual authorities, but the Mind of the Church which never varies from age to age, and which is articulated solely in her infallible Magisterium.

For this reason, I have declined to elaborate on the personal opinions of those apologetes which might serve to contradict the formal teaching of the Catholic Church; just as, for example, if I were composing an article on the sinlessness of our Blessed Mother, I would choose to ignore as authoritative the erroneous statements of those seven canonized Doctors of the Church - St. Thomas Aquinas, St. Bernard of Clairvaux, St. Bonaventure, St. Peter Damian, St. Albert the Great, St. Anselm of Canterbury, and St. John Damascene - each of whom controverted the Dogma of the Immaculate Conception. Instead, I have made every effort simply to provide as many references as possible which conspicuously align themselves with the Magisterium and Mind of the Church in the consistency of her Analogy of Faith.

In this, I believe that I am not only supporting the true doctrine of Christ as proclaimed throughout the ages by the voice of His Church, but likewise protecting the mutual integrity of all the sainted spokesmen of that Church who have swelled the chorus of her clarion call to men of every clime and time. Therefore, should some skeptic insist on following any theological witness in contradistinction to what has come down to us in the Deposit of Faith and is officially interpreted solely by the Church as the Word and Revelation of God Himself, let him be made aware that he is following, not what the Church infallibly teaches, but mere personal opinion based on the word of man. Not the Catholic Faith, but speculation thereon. Not the Revelation of God, but the "tradition of men" and the "leaven of Pharisees" (Mk. 7:8; 8:15) against which Our Lord Himself inveighed and admonished us. For, all the most ingenious hypotheses in the world do not one single dogma make. Moreover, when they serve to contradict or to cast doubt upon defined dogmas of Faith, such postulations are not permitted to be held even privately.

Nevertheless, to those who persist in supporting the conjecture of any individual, even the most brilliant, against the formal declaration of the Magisterium, I need only reiterate the condemnation of error decreed by Pope Alexander VIII against the Jansenists that, should anyone find a teaching clearly established by a Father or a Doctor of the Church, even one as eminent as St. Augustine, he may absolutely hold and teach it in disregard of papal pronouncement (DNZ 1320). Indeed, history proves that every Father of the Church has at one time or another published errors which later had to be condemned by the Church. The Pope of Rome, when speaking infallibly, never errs. Hence, in quoting our sources and authorities only when they substantiate the Holy Father in the fullness of his office as Supreme Teacher and Shepherd, we are not being arbitrary, nor unethical. We are being *Catholic*.

As for the lesser lights in this collection, their testimony is all the more conclusive, not because it likely caught them in some unguarded moment of orthodoxy, but because it demonstrates convincingly that these witnesses have all said the same identical thing, and said it over, and over, and over again. The sense of dogma remains always the same, since the Mind of the Church never changes in its regard. The truth speaks for itself, and forcefully so. "I am the truth," Jesus declares to us; and thus, "Whosoever is of the truth hears My voice" (Jn. 14:6; 18:37).

Michael Malone

FEAST OF THE CHAIR OF ST. PETER
February 22, 1993

11

APOSTOLIC DIGEST: BOOK I

The
BOOK OF MARY

DEVOTION TO OUR LADY
IS NECESSARY FOR SALVATION

In me is all hope of life and of virtue, in me is all grace of the way and the truth.
Ecclesiasticus 24:25

All the saints have a great devotion to Our Lady: no grace comes from Heaven without passing through her hands. We cannot go into a house without speaking to the door-keeper. Well, the Holy Virgin is the doorkeeper of Heaven. ***John Mary Vianney***

All gifts, virtues, and graces of the Holy Ghost are administered by the hands of Mary to whomsoever she desires, when she desires, in the manner she desires, and to whatever degree she desires. Mary is the dispensatrix of all the graces God bestows. Every grace granted to man in this life has three successive steps: from God it comes to Christ, and from Christ to the Virgin, and from the Virgin it descends to us. ***St. Bernardine of Siena***

Every grace which is communicated has a three-fold origin: it flows from God to Christ, from Christ to the Virgin, and from the Virgin to us.

Pope Leo XIII

The Lord has placed in Mary the plenitude of all good so that, if any hope of grace or salvation is in us, we know that we derive it all from Mary.

St. Bernard

For this reason, all creatures are obligated to render her respect and homage, as to their Queen and Sovereign to whom they belong, and upon whom they depend, and will depend, for all eternity.

St. John Eudes

Even as Eve, having become disobedient, was made the cause of death both to herself and to the entire human reace, so also did Mary, by being obedient, become the cause of salvation both to herself and to the whole human race. And therefore, as the human race was made subject to death by a virgin, so is it saved by a virgin. *St. Irenaeus of Lyons*

Mary has the greatest and clearest claims to our homage and praise: she is the salvation of the world; our dependence upon the august Mary is complete and universal. There is neither on earth nor in Heaven any justified soul, any one of the Elect, who does not owe Mary his justice and his glory.

Ven. William Joseph Chaminade

Many have proved invincibly, from the sentiments of the Fathers - among others: St. Augustine, St. Ephem, St. Cyril of Jerusalem, St. Germanus of Conantinople, St. John Damascene, St. Anselm, St. Bernard, St. Bernardine, St. Thomas, and St. Bonaventure - that devotion to Our Most Blessed Virgin is necessary for salvation, and that it is an infallible mark of reprobation to have no esteem or love for the Holy Virgin while, on the other hand, it is an infallible mark of predestination to be entirely and truly devoted to her.   *St. Louis Marie de Montfort*

If our life were not under the protection of Mary, we might tremble for our perseverance and salvation. In her hands Jesus has placed His almighty power in the order of salvation. All the graces of salvation, both the natural and the spiritual, will be given to us by Mary.   *St. Peter Julian Eymard*

Mary is the whole hope of our salvation.
                              St. Thomas Aquinas

The foundation of all our confidence is found in the Blessed Virgin Mary. Through her are obtained every hope, every grace, and all salvation. For this is God's will: that we obtain everything through Mary.
                              Ven. Pope Pius IX

A mediator, then, was needed with the Mediator Himself, nor could a more fitting one be found than Mary.   *St. Bernard*

Mary is our necessary and universal Mediatrix. No one can go to the Son but by Mary, just as no one can go to the Father but by the Son. Only through Mary do we reach Jesus, since Jesus came to us only through Mary.   *Ven. William Joseph Chaminade*

Nothing comes to us except through the mediation of Mary, for such is the will of God. *Pope Leo XIII*

To reach the Eternal Father, we must go to Jesus, our Mediator of Redemption. To go to Jesus, we must go to Mary, our Mediatrix of Intercession.

St. Louis Marie de Montfort

What, therefore, God hath joined together, let no man put asunder ... Take the Child *and* His Mother.

St. Matthew 19:4; 2:20

The Child is not found without Mary, His Mother. If, then, it is impossible to separate what God has united, it is also certain that you cannot find Jesus except with Mary and through Mary.

Pope St. Pius X

We must never separate Jesus from Mary; we can go to Him only through her. Without Mary, we would never find Jesus. Whoever would say "I have no need of Mary" would be guilty of blasphemy! Our eternal salvation is at stake, and we are bound to honor her as the Mother of God and our Mother.

St. Peter Julian Eymard

Mary is the Ark of God, the center of the universe, the cause of creation, the business of the ages. Towards her turn the men who have gone before us, we who are now living, those who are to follow us, our children's children, and their descendants. If we have any chance of salvation, we have it all from Mary. Go, then, have recourse to Mary.

St. Bernard

THOSE DEVOTED TO OUR LADY SHALL OBTAIN SALVATION

He who shall find me shall find life and shall have salvation from the Lord.
Proverbs 8:35

If you persevere till death in true devotion to Mary, your salvation is certain.
St. Alphonsus Maria Liguori

With reason did the Most Holy Virgin predict that all generations would call her blessed, for all the Elect obtain eternal salvation through the means of Mary.
St. Idelphonsus

Christ entrusted to His Mother's maternal care the mission of making the Church a single family. Yes, in Mary we have the bond of communion for all of us who, through Faith and Baptism, are disciples and brothers of Jesus.
Pope John Paul II

In the multitude of the Elect she shall have praise, and among the blessed she shall be blessed.
Ecclesiasticus 24:4

Her children rose up and called her blessed.
Proverbs 31:28

For behold, from henceforth all generations shall call me blessed ... who are born not of blood, nor of the will of the flesh, nor of man, but of God.

St. Luke 1:48; St. John 1:13

O Mary, thou art blessed among women, for thou hast brought forth life for both men and women!

St. Augustine

Every one of the multitudes, therefore, whom the evil of calamitous circumstances has stolen away from Catholic unity, must be born again to Christ by that same Mother whom God has endowed with a never-failing fertility to bring forth a holy people.

Pope Leo XIII

Bearing in her womb the Savior, Mary can also be said to have borne all those whose life the Savior's life enshrined. All of us, then, as many as are knit to Christ, have come forth from Mary's womb: one Body, as it were, knit together with its Head.

Pope St. Pius X

Although in the most pure womb of Mary there was but one kernel of grain, Jesus Christ, nevertheless, her womb is called a "heap of wheat" (Cant. 7:2) because all the Elect were virtually contained in it.

St. Ambrose

Mary is that Happy Ark, in which those who take refuge will never suffer the shipwreck of eternal perdition.

St. Bernard

However great a sinner may have been, if he shows himself devout to Mary he will never perish.

St. Hilary of Poitiers

Souls protected by Mary, and on whom she casts her eyes, are necessarily justified and saved. Just as it is impossible that they be saved from whom Mary turns away her eyes of mercy, so it is certain that they who are loved by Mary, and for whom she intercedes, will obtain justification and eternal life.

St. Antoninus

We believe that Mary opens the abyss of God's mercy to whomsoever she wills, when she wills, and as she wills; so that there is no sinner, however great, who is lost if Mary protects him.

St. Bonaventure

He who is devout to the Virgin Mother will certainly never be lost. *St. Ignatius of Antioch*

Not a single soul who has really persevered in her service has ever been damned.

St. Louis Marie de Montfort

O Mother of God! If I place my confidence in thee, I shall be saved; if I am under thy protection, I have nothing to fear; for being thy client is a certainty of salvation which God grants *only* to those whom He intends to save. *St. John Damascene*

Being thy servant, O Mary, is a surety of salvation which God grants solely to those He will save.

St. Andrew of Crete

The servants of Mary are as certain of getting to Paradise as though they were already there. Who are they who are saved, and reign in Heaven? Surely, those for whom the Queen of Mercy intercedes. The clients of Mary will *necessarily* be saved!

St. Alphonsus Maria Liguori

O Blessed Mary, whoever loves you, honors God; whoever serves you, pleases God; whoever invokes your holy name, with a pure heart, will infallibly receive the object of his petition.   *St. Bernard*

O admirable Mother of God! How many sins have I committed for which thou hast obtained pardon for me, and how many others would I have committed if thou hadst not preserved me? How often have I seen myself on the brink of Hell in obvious danger of falling into it but for thy most benign hand which saved me? Alas! Without thee, my dearest and all-good Mother, where should I be today? I should be in the fiery furnace of Hell!   *St. John Eudes*

Would that everyone might know that I would already be damned already were it not for Mary!

St. Louis Marie de Montfort

THOSE WHO REFUSE TO HONOR OUR LADY WILL BE LOST

He who angers His Mother
is cursed by God.
Ecclesiasticus 3:18

The honor of Mary is so intimately connected with the honor and glory of Jesus that to deny the one is at the same time a denial of the other.
Ven. William Joseph Chaminade

He who neglects the service of the Blessed Virgin will die in his sins. He who does not invoke thee, O Lady, will never get to Heaven. Not only will those from whom Mary turns her countenance not be saved, but there will be no hope of their salvation. No one can be saved without the protection of the Blessed Virgin Mary.   **St. Bonaventure**

To desire grace without recourse to the Virgin Mother is to desire to fly without wings. **Pope Pius XII**

If you would enter into Life, keep the commandments ... Honor thy father and thy mother.
St. Matthew 19:17,19

Behold thy Mother!   **St. John 19:27**

Jesus honored her before all ages, and will honor her for all ages. No one comes to Him, nor even near Him, no one is saved or sanctified, if he too will not honor her. This is the lot of angels and of men.

St. Maximilian Mary Kolbe

There is a generation that does not bless their Mother, a generation pure in their own eyes and yet not washed from their filthiness.   *Proverbs 30:11-12*

All the true children of God, the predestinate, have God for their Father and Mary for their Mother. He who has not Mary for his Mother has not God for his Father.   *St. Louis Marie de Montfort*

Whoever does not wish to have Mary Immaculate as his Mother will not have Christ as his Brother either; the Father will not send His Son to him; the Son will not descend into his soul; the Holy Spirit will not make him a member of the Mystical Body of Christ; for all these mysteries of grace take place in Mary Full-of-Grace, and in her alone. And, since the First-Born Son was conceived only through the specific consent of the Most Blessed Virgin, the same holds true for all other humans.

St. Maximilian Mary Kolbe

Your heart will either sing the divine canticles of Our Lady, or echo the cursed and unhappy songs of worldlings here in dishonor to God and vibrate eternally with the blasphemies and horrid dirges of the damned in Hell!   *St. John Eudes*

APOSTOLIC DIGEST: BOOK II

The
BOOK OF
SALVATION

THERE IS NO SALVATION OUTSIDE THE ONE TRUE CHURCH

The Lord added daily to the Church those who would be saved.
Acts of the Apostles 2:47

The Church is One, Holy, Catholic, Apostolic, and *Roman*: unique, the Chair founded on Peter. Outside her fold is to be found neither the true faith nor eternal salvation, for it is impossible to have God for a Father if one does not have the Church for a Mother. **Ven. Pope Pius IX**

There is only one universal Church of the faithful, outside which there is absolutely no salvation. **IV Lateran Council**

The House of God is but one, and no one can have salvation except in the Church. **St. Cyprian**

Whosoever would be saved, let him come into this House. Let no one talk himself out of it; let no one deceive himself: outside this House, that is, outside the Church, no one is saved. **Origen**

It is a *sin* to believe there is salvation outside the Catholic Church! **Ven. Pope Pius IX**

If any man does not enter the Church, or if any man departs from it, he is far from the hope of life and salvation. *Pope Pius XI*

There is no salvation outside the Catholic Church. Anyone who resists this truth perishes.
St. Louis Marie de Montfort

Where is the road which leads us to Jesus Christ? It is the Church. It is our duty to recall to everyone, great and small, the absolute necessity we are under to have recourse to this Church in order to work out our eternal salvation. *Pope St. Pius X*

There is but one plain known road. When you wander from this, you are lost. You must be altogether within the House of God, within the walls of salvation, to be sound and safe from injury. If you wander and walk abroad ever so little, if you carelessly thrust hand or foot out of the Ship, you shall be thrust forth: the door is shut, the ocean roars, you are undone. *St. Edmund Campion*

Anyone who is out of the Ship is walking a path not to Heaven, but to Hell. He is hurrying to the torment of eternal death! *St. Fulgentius*

There is only one Catholic Church; this we firmly believe and profess without qualification. Outside this Church there is no salvation and no remission of sins. For at the time of the Deluge there existed only one Ark, the figure of the one Church. And all things outside this Ark perished. *Pope Boniface VIII*

It must be held as a matter of faith that outside the Apostolic Roman Church no one can be saved, that the Church is the only Ark of Salvation, and that whoever does not enter it will perish in the Flood.

Ven. Pope Pius IX

There is no entering into salvation outside of the Church, just as in the time of the Deluge there was none outside the Ark which denotes the Church.

Pope John Paul II

The Ship of the Church is guided by Christ and His Vicar. It alone carries the disciples, and receives Christ. Yes, it is tossed on the sea, but outside it one would perish immediately. Salvation is solely in the Church; outside it one perishes.   *Pope John Paul I*

I profess that outside the Catholic Church no one is saved.   *Pope Sylvester II*

O glorious St. Peter, obtain for us a sincere loyalty to our Holy Mother the Church; grant that we may ever remain most closely and sincerely united to the Roman Pontiff who is the heir of thy faith and authority: the one, true, visible head of the Catholic Church, that mystical Ark outside which there is no salvation.   *Pope Benedict XV*

SALVATION IS FOUND ONLY IN THE CATHOLIC CHURCH

Christ is the Savior of His Body.
Ephesians 5:23

The Catholic Church alone is the Body of Christ, of which He is Head and Savior. The "People of God" and the "Mystical Body of Christ" are one and the same thing, both of them designating *the Church.* Membership in the Church requires conditions other than Baptism alone; it requires identical faith and unity of communion, so that by means of the Catholic Church alone, which is the unrestricted instrument of salvation, is it possible to obtain the fulness of the means to salvation. Indeed, the Church is both a sure and an exclusive means of attaining salvation. We must always remember the unity of the Mystical Body outside which there is no salvation, for there is no entering into salvation outside the Church. Outside this Body, the Holy Spirit gives life to no one: those who are enemies to unity do not participate in the charity of Divine Life; those outside the Church do not possess the Holy Spirit. The entrance to salvation is open to no one outside the Church!

Pope Paul VI

The Church alone is the entrance to salvation.

Pope Pius XII

27

By means of religious indifference, crafty men deceitfully pretend that people can attain eternal salvation in the practice of any religion. They conclude that others, however estranged from Catholic unity, are equally on the road to salvation and that they are able to achieve everlasting life. Words fail us from utter horror in detesting and abhorring this new and terrible insult! *Ven. Pope Pius IX*

When it is a question of life and salvation, we must say of the Church what St. Peter said of Jesus Christ Himself: "Neither is there salvation in any other" (Acts 4:12). *Pope Pius XI*

The mystery of salvation is continued and accomplished in the Church, and from this single source it reaches the whole world. *There is no salvation outside the Church.* From her alone there flows the life-giving force destined to renew the whole of humanity, directing every human being to become a part of the Mystical Body of Christ. *Pope John Paul II*

All who desire eternal salvation must cling to the Church and embrace her, like those who entered the Ark to escape perishing in the Flood.
Catechism of Trent

Whoever is separated from this Catholic Church, no matter how much he believes he is living praiseworthily, will not have life, but the anger of God rests upon him. The reason is this offense alone: that he is sundered from the unity of Christ.
St. Augustine

He who does not keep the true Catholic faith whole and without error will undoubtedly be lost. He who is separated from the Catholic Church will not have life.   *Pope Gregory XVI*

Cut off from the Body into which alone the graces of Christ flow, you are deprived of the benefit of all prayers, sacrifices, and Sacraments. You will gain nothing except perhaps to be tortured somewhat less horribly in the everlasting fire than Judas, or Luther, or Zwingli.   *St. Edmund Campion*

There is nothing a Christian should dread more than to be separated from the Body of Christ; for, if separated, he is not one of His members. And, since no one can ascend into Heaven but him who has become His member in His Body, the saying is fulfilled that "No one ascends into Heaven except Him Who descended" (Jn. 3:13).   *St. Augustine*

There is salvation in no one except Christ, and the Church is His Body.   *Pope John Paul II*

That the Mystical Body of Christ and the Catholic Church in communion with Rome are one and the same thing is a doctrine based on Revealed Truth. That we must necessarily belong to the true Church if we are to attain everlasting salvation is a statement which some people reduce to a meaningless formula.
                                              Pope Pius XII

It is impossible to be joined to God except through Jesus Christ; it is impossible to be united to Christ except in and through the Church, His Mystical Body. *Pope John XXIII*

The union of Christ with the members of the Mystical Body is obtained only by membership in the Church, for outside this chaste Spouse there is no union with the Bridegroom. There is no life outside the Church because all the life that is to be had can come only from her, and no one possesses this life unless he belongs to her. Outside the Church there is no salvation. *Ven. William Joseph Chaminade*

Those who acknowledge Christ must acknowledge Him completely and entirely. The Head is the only-begotten Son of God; the Body is His Church. No one can in any way be counted among the children of God unless they take Jesus Christ as their Brother and, at the same time, the Church as their Mother. Christianity is, in fact, incarnate in the Catholic Church; it is identified with that perfect spiritual society which is the Mystical Body of Jesus Christ and has for its visible head the Roman Pontiff. Consequently, all who wish to reach salvation outside the Church are mistaken as to the way and are engaged in a futile effort. This is our last lesson to you; receive it, engrave it upon your minds, all of you: by God's commandment *salvation is to be found nowhere but in the Church. Pope Leo XIII*

CHAPTER THREE

THOSE OUTSIDE THE CATHOLIC CHURCH ARE LOST FOREVER

If anyone abide not in Me, he shall be cast forth as a branch, and shall wither, and they shall gather him up and cast him into the fire, and he burneth.   *St. John 15:6*

The most Holy Roman Church believes, professes, and teaches that none of those who are not within the Catholic Church, not only pagans, but also Jews, and heretics, and schismatics, can ever have a share in eternal life, but that they will go into the everlasting fire prepared for the devil and his angels unless before death they shall have entered into the Church; and that so important is the unity of this ecclesiastical body that only those abiding within this unity can profit from the Sacraments of the Church unto salvation, and that they alone can receive an eternal reward for their fasts, their almsgiving, their other works of Christian piety and duties of a Christian soldier. No one, let his almsgiving be as great as it may be, no one, even if he pour out his blood for the name of Christ, can be saved unless he abide within the bosom and unity of the Catholic Church.

Pope Eugene IV

He who is separated from the body of the Catholic Church, however praiseworthy his conduct may otherwise seem, will not be saved.

Pope Gregory XVI

Not one man of those outside the faith and obedience to the Pontiff of the Romans can finally be saved.

Pope Clement VI

Whoever does not preserve this unity does not preserve the law of God, does not preserve the faith of the Father and Son, and does not have life and salvation.

Pope Pius XII

We must believe that the Roman Catholic Church is the only true Church; hence, they who are out of our Church, or they who are separated from it, cannot be saved.

St. Alphonsus Maria Liguori

Outside the fold of the Holy Roman Church there is no salvation.

Ven. Pope Pius IX

This is the Holy Church, the One Church, the True Church, the Catholic Church, fighting against all heresies! He will not have God for his Father who refuses the Church for his Mother. No one can find salvation except in the Catholic Church. Outside the Church, you can find everything except salvation. You can have dignities, you can have Sacraments, you can sing "Alleluia," answer "Amen," have the Gospels, have faith and preach it, too. But never can you find salvation except in the Catholic Church.

St. Augustine

No one can be saved outside the bosom and unity of the Catholic Church.　　　*Council of Florence*

Outside this communion, as outside the Ark of Noah, there is absolutely no salvation for mortals; for the rule of Cyprian and Augustine is certain: that man will not have God for his Father who would not have the Church for his Mother. *St. Peter Canisius*

Our Lord said that whoever would not listen to the Church should be regarded as a heathen. He said that there was to be but one flock and one shepherd, and He appointed St. Peter to be head of that flock. My friend, there are not two ways of serving Our Lord; there is only one good way, and it is to serve Him as He wishes to be served.
　　　　　　　　　St. John Mary Vianney

Oh, how much are worldlings deceived who think to go to Heaven by the wide way that only leadeth to perdition! The path to Heaven is narrow, rough, and full of wearisome ascents, nor can it be trodden without great toil. And therefore, wrong is their way, gross their error, and assured their ruin who, after the testimony of so many thousands of saints, will not learn where to settle their footing! Wrestle no longer against the struggles of your own conscience and the forcible admonitions God doth send you. Embrace His mercy before the time of rigor, and return to His Church lest He debar you His Kingdom. He cannot have God for Father who refuseth to possess the Catholic Church for Mother.
　　　　　　　　　St. Robert Southwell

The exaltation of Holy Church is our exaltation, for in no other place do souls receive life than in that Church. No one can attain to joy in the beauty of God without the help of that sweet Bride, for we must all pass through the gate of Christ Crucified, and that gate is found nowhere but in the Church.

St. Catherine of Siena

Hold most firmly and do not doubt at all: not only all the pagans, but also all the Jews and all the heretics and schismatics who terminate this present life outside the Catholic Church will go into the everlasting fire prepared for the devil and his angels.

St. Fulgentius

To that Church alone, and to those whom she embraces in her bosom and holds in her arms, appertains the invocation of that Divine Name, outside which there is no other name under Heaven given to men whereby we must be saved.

Catechism of Trent

O Mary, Mother of Mercy and Seat of Wisdom! Enlighten the minds enfolded in the darkness of ignorance and sin, that they may clearly recognize the Holy, Catholic, Apostolic, Roman Church to be the only true Church of Jesus Christ, outside which neither sanctity nor salvation can be found. *Pope Pius XII*

APOSTOLIC DIGEST: BOOK III

The
BOOK OF FAITH

THERE IS NO SALVATION EXCEPT IN THE CATHOLIC FAITH

Without faith, it is impossible to please God. *Hebrews 11:6*

We must first turn our attention towards that faith without which it is impossible to please God. You know well with what constancy our Fathers endeavored to inculcate this Article of Faith which innovators dare to deny: the necessity of the Catholic faith and Catholic unity to obtain salvation.

Pope Gregory XVI

Since without faith it is impossible to please God, no one is justified without it, nor will anyone attain eternal life unless he perseveres to the end in it.

I Vatican Council

Without the faith, no one is ever justified.

Council of Trent

When we say that faith is necessary for the remission of sins, we mean to speak of the *Catholic* faith, not heretical faith. Without the habit of this faith, no man is justified.   *St. Alphonsus Maria Liguori*

Unless a man keeps this faith whole and entire, he shall undoubtedly be lost.   *Ven. Pope Pius IX*

Whoever wishes to be saved needs, above everything else, to hold the Catholic faith. Unless each one preserves this faith whole and inviolate, he will perish in eternity without a doubt. *Pope Eugene IV*

The first requirement of salvation is to keep to the standard of the true faith. *Pope Adrian II*

See to it that the faithful have fixed firmly in their minds this dogma of our most holy religion: the absolute necessity of the Catholic faith for attaining salvation. *Ven. Pope Pius IX*

Remember this firm dogma of our religion: that outside the true Catholic faith no one can be saved. *Pope Pius VIII*

No one can depart from the teaching of Catholic truth without loss of faith and salvation. *Pope Pius XII*

No one can be saved outside this true Catholic faith. *Pope Gregory XIII*

I will go peaceably and firmly to the Catholic Church. For if faith is so important, I will seek it where true faith first began, among those who received it from God Himself. It is a curious contradiction of principles which allows every sect that can obtain a name to be right and in the way of salvation! *St. Elizabeth Ann Seton*

My faith is the true faith; it is the right faith; it is the faith that leads to Heaven. I was born in that faith, and in that faith I mean to die. But you, be converted and do penance. Give up your schism and submit to our Holy Father, or you will never save your soul!
St. Andrew Bobola

The knowledge of the dogmas of the faith of Christ is necessary for every one who earnestly desires the salvation of his soul. *St. Robert Bellarmine*

The truth of our faith is established by so many manifest proofs that he who does not embrace it can only be called a fool. *St. Alphonsus Maria Liguori*

Without this faith no one can enter the kingdom of Heaven. *St. Bede the Venerable*

Hold fast, then, brethren, to the true, the genuine, the Catholic faith. This is our faith: the true faith, the right faith, the Catholic faith which comes, not from private judgment, but from the testimony of the Scriptures; not based on faltering heretical rashness but on Apostolic truth. *St. Augustine*

Whoever wishes to be saved must, above all, keep the Catholic faith; for, unless a person keeps this faith whole and entire, he will undoubtedly be lost forever. This is the Catholic faith: everyone must believe it firmly and steadfastly, otherwise he cannot be saved. *The Athanasian Creed*

The words are not mine, but God's and the Apostles' and Prophets' who have never lied: "He who believes shall be saved, but he who does not believe shall be damned" (Mk. 16:16). God hath spoken!

St. Patrick

And all of us humbly entreat and beseech everyone, all nations and all men in all the earth who are, and who shall be, that we may all of us persevere in the true faith: for otherwise no one can be saved.

St. Francis of Assisi

Constantly hold and profess this true Catholic faith, without which no one can be saved.

Council of Trent

I promise, vow, and swear that, with God's help, I shall most constantly hold and profess this true Catholic faith, outside which no one can be saved.

Pope Pius IV

This true Catholic faith, outside which no one can be saved, which I now freely profess and truly hold, I do promise and swear that I will most constantly keep and confess whole and inviolate with the help of God until the last breath of my life, and that I will take great care that it be held, taught, and preached by my inferiors and by those who are placed under my charge. *Papal Oath: I Vatican Council*

ALL INFIDELS WILL BE DAMNED IN ETERNITY

The unbelieving will have their portion in the pool burning with fire and brimstone.
Apocalypse 21:8

Persist in the true faith and ground your life on the rock of the Church, lest your many tears and good works avail you nothing, separated from the true faith. Works, however good they may seem, are nothing if separated from the solidarity of the faith.
Pope St. Gregory the Great

Wherefore, let us be fruitful, not in paganism, not in Judaism, not in any evil heresy, but in the House of God; for ungodly men bring forth fruits in vain outside the Church.
St. Nilus

Assuredly, such people possess a certain kind of goodness; but, because it is not the product of faith in God nor love of God, it is not able to help them.
St. Fulgentius

To have merit, each act must not only be a natural work, but also a supernatural work; and this cannot be said of the infidel who, because he is without the faith, cannot perform supernatural good works.
St. Alphonsus Maria Liguori

Well should the pagan weep and lament who, not knowing God, goes straight to punishment when he dies! *St. John Chrysostom*

If you die as an unbeliever, you will be damned and lost forever. *St. John Bosco*

Whoever does not embrace the Catholic Christian religion will be damned, as was Mohammed.
St. Peter Mavimenus

Mohammed was a disciple of the devil, and his followers are in a state of perdition.
St. George of San Saba

We can no more pray for a deceased infidel than we can for the devil, since they are condemned to the same eternal and irrevocable damnation.
Pope St. Gregory the Great

Those who die as infidels are damned.
Pope St. Pius X

Where knowledge of the eternal and unchangeable Truth is lacking, there is only false virtue even with the best of conduct. For, without worship of the true God, even what might seem to be virtue is sin.
St. Prosper of Aquitaine

Unbelief is a mortal sin. *Council of Trent*

Is unbelief a mortal sin? Listen to Our Lord: "If you do not believe that I am He, you shall die in your sins!" (Jn. 8:24). *St. Benedict Joseph Labre*

O ye atheists who do not believe in God, what fools you are! But if you do believe there is a God, you must also believe there is a true religion. And if not the Roman Catholic, which is? Perhaps that of the pagans who admit many gods, and thus deny them all. Perhaps that of Mohammed, a religion invented by an imposter and framed for beasts rather than humans. Perhaps that of the Jews who had the true faith at one time but, because they rejected their Redeemer, lost their faith, their country, their everything. Perhaps that of heretics who, separating themselves our Church, have confused all revealed dogmas in such a way that the belief of one heretic is contrary to that of his neighbor. O holy faith! Enlighten all those poor blind creatures who run to eternal perdition! *St. Alphonsus Maria Liguori*

O eternal God, remember that the souls of infidels have been created by Thee after Thine own image and likeness. Behold, Lord, how to the dishonor of Thy name, Hell is peopled with them! Forget their idolatry and infidelity, and grant that they may at length acknowledge Our Lord Jesus Christ in Whom is our salvation. *St. Francis Xavier*

CHAPTER THREE

ALL HERETICS ARE IN
A STATE OF PERDITION

*Whosoever revolts, and continues not
in the doctrine of Christ, has not God.*
II St. John 1:9

If anyone does not profess properly and truthfully all
that has been handed down and taught publicly to
the Holy, Catholic, and Apostolic Church of God, to
the last detail in word and intention: let him be anathema. *I Lateran Council*

If anyone does not with mind and lips reject and anathematize all abominable heretics together with their
impious writings, even to the single least portion, let
such a person be condemned. *Pope St. Martin I*

They have gone forth from us, but were not of us.
For if they had been of us, they would surely have
continued with us. Whosoever does not continue in
the doctrine of Christ does not have God.
St. John I, 2:19; II, 1:9

Whoever withdraws and departs from the Church
will be guilty, even though he has attained grace in
the Church. That he will perish will be imputed to
himself. *St. Cyprian*

Thou art a God Who hatest all the workers of iniquity: Thou wilt destroy all who speak a lie. *Psalm 5:7*

You heretics are all guilty and wicked by the crime of schism. From this most heinous sacrilege not one of you can say he is innocent.   *St. Augustine*

He who to support heresy distorts the Sacred Scriptures from their genuine and true meaning is guilty of the greatest injury to the Word of God; and against this crime we are warned by the Prince of the Apostles: "There are certain things hard to be understood, which the unlearned and unstable wrest, as they also do other Scriptures, to their own destruction" (II Peter 3:16).   *Catechism of Trent*

The unbelief of heretics, who confess their belief in the Gospel and resist that faith by corrupting it, is a more grievous sin than that of the heathens, because the heathens have not accepted the faith in any way at all. Hence, the unbelief of heretics is the worst sin. Speaking absolutely, the unbelief of heretics is worse than that of pagans or Jews.   *St. Thomas Aquinas*

The greatest evil existing today is heresy, an infernal rage which hurls countless souls into eternal damnation.   *St. John Eudes*

These unfortunate people do not see that, in refusing to submit to the Church, they reduce themselves to believing in nothing. The so-called Reformers have revived ancient heresies, and have sought by false doctrines to destroy the faith of Jesus Christ, and, if possible, to bring all souls with themselves to eternal perdition. *St. Alphonsus Maria Liguori*

Protestantism is the Great Revolt against God.
Ven. Pope Pius IX

Heretics are Antichrists and adversaries of Christ.
VII Council of Carthage

Heretics are to be classed with thieves and murderers. *Pope Innocent IV*

Hence, if you fear to leave this Catholic unity outside which there is no salvation, beware of the subtleties of heretics. *Ven Pope Pius IX*

Therefore, let the blind and foolish subtlety of heretical impiety be despised. Whosoever continues in heresy is unpardonable, nor can he ever attain forgiveness. They are falling into that blasphemy which shall never be forgiven, neither in this world nor in the Judgment to come. *Pope St. Leo the Great*

Those who have been detected *even by slight proof* to have deviated from the doctrine of the Catholic religion ought to fall under the classification of heretic and under the sentences operating against heretics. *Pope Innocent IV*

If anyone holds to a single heresy, he is not a Catholic. *St. Augustine*

What is the use of fighting for many articles of the faith, and to perish for the doubting of a few? He be-

45

lieves no one article of faith who refuses to believe any single one. *St. Edmund Campion*

Against the First Commandment, all those sin who do not have faith. Such sinners are very numerous, for they include all wh fall into heresy, all who reject what Holy Mother the Church proposes for our belief. *Catechism of Trent*

Anyone who says "I love God," and does not keep His commandments, is a liar.
Pope St. Gregory the Great

Those who turn aside unto deceits, the Lord shall number with the workers of iniquity. Thou art a God Who hatest all the workers of iniquity: Thou wilt destroy all who speak a lie. *Psalm 124:5; 5:7*

A man who is a heretic is subverted and sins, being condemned by his own judgment. *St. Titus 3:10-11*

Heresies are embraced only by those who, had they persevered in the faith, would be lost by the irregularity of their lives. *St. Augustine*

What shows me that your life is badly governed? The poison of heresy! You have deserted the light and gone into darkness! I beg that you delay no more, nor kick against the prick of conscience which I know is perpetually tormenting you. Return, return, and do not wait for the rod of justice. For our faults do not pass unpunished, especially those committed against Holy Church. *St. Catherine of Siena*

Many Protestants have almost the same practices as we, only they do not submit to the Holy Father and attach themselves to the true Ark of Salvation. They do not want to become Catholics and unite themselves under the banner of truth wherein alone there is true salvation. Of what avail is it, children, if Protestants lead naturally pure, honest lives, yet lack the Holy Ghost? They may well say: "We do no harm; we lead good lives"; but, if they do not enter the true fold of Christ, all their protestations are in vain.

St. Frances Xavier Cabrini

People often say, "It is better to be a good Protestant than a bad Catholic." That is not true! That would mean that one could be saved without the true faith. No. A bad Catholic remains a child of the family, although a prodigal; and however great a sinner he may be, he still has a right to mercy. Through his faith, a bad Catholic is nearer to God than a Protestant, for he is a member of the household, whereas the heretic is not. And how hard it is to make him become one! *St. Peter Julian Eymard*

How many are the infidels, heretics, and schismatics who do not enjoy the happiness of the true faith! The earth is full of them, and they are all lost!

St. Alphonsus Maria Liguori

Therefore, we are right in censuring, anathematizing, abhorring, and abominating the perversity of heart shown by heretics. *St. Augustine*

We excommunicate and anathematize every heresy, condemning all heretics under whatever names they may be known; for, while they have different faces, they are nevertheless bound to each other by their tails. Secular authorities shall be compelled to exterminate all heretics to the best of their ability, and if, from sufficient evidence, it is apparent that a bishop is negligent in cleansing his diocese of heretical wickedness, let him be deposed and another substituted who will confound heretical depravity. But if any of them by damnable obstinacy disapprove, from this very fact let *them* be regarded as heretics.

IV Lateran Council

I could go forth all by myself against miserable heretics! *St. Teresa of Avila*

How happy I would have been to fight at the time of the Crusades or, later on, against the heretics! I want to be a warrior, a martyr! Oh! Is it possible I must die in *bed*? *St. Therese of Lisieux*

A Christian should argue with a blasphemer only by running his sword through his bowels as far as it will go. *St. Louis, King of France*

When a person blasphemes, his mouth should instantly be shut. Strike him in the mouth! Crush it, so that he cannot speak! *St. John Chrysostom*

THE ONCE-CHOSEN PEOPLE
ARE NOW THE ACCURSED RACE

Christ shall be slain, and the people
who shall deny Him shall not be His.
Daniel 9:26

The Gentiles have attained to justice, but Israel has not come unto the law of justice. Why? Because they sought it not by faith, for they stumbled at the Stumbing Stone. **Romans 9:30-32**

Our Lord Jesus Christ referred to Himself as "the Stone" (Mt. 21:44). Lying on the ground, it shakes whoever falls over it; coming from on high, it crushes the proud. The Jews have already been shaken by their previous stumble. What awaits them is to be crushed by His Coming. *St. Augustine*

Christ is the Stone which was rejected which has become the cornerstone: nor is there salvation in any other. For, there is no other name under Heaven whereby we must be saved. *Acts 4:10-12*

Many shall come from the East and the West, and sit down in the kingdom of Heaven, but the children of the kingdom shall be cast out, into the exterior darkness: there shall be weeping and gnashing of teeth. *St. Matthew 8:11-12*

Early and often did the Lord send His messengers to them, for He had compassion on His people. But they mocked the messengers of God, despised His warnings, and scoffed at His prophets, till the anger of the Lord against His people was so inflamed that there was no remedy.   *II Paralipomenon 36:15-16*

Therefore, I say to you: the kingdom of God shall be taken away from you, and given to a nation yielding the fruits thereof.   *St. Matthew 21:43*

Do not add to your sins by saying that the Covenant is both theirs and ours. Yes, it is ours, but they lost it forever.   *St. Barnabas*

Christ annuls the First Covenant to establish the Second. For, if that First Covenant had been faultless, then there would be no place for the Second. They did not persevere in My Covenant, saith the Lord, and I disregarded them. *Hebrews 10:9; 8:7-9*

So clearly was the transition then made from the Synagogue to the Church that, when the Lord gave up His soul, the veil of the Temple was rent in two.
Pope St. Leo the Great

Since His spouse, the Synagogue, refused to receive Him, Christ answered: "This is a harlot!" and gave her a bill of divorce.   *St. Vincent Ferrer*

Dreadful are the ends of a wicked race!
Wisdom 3:19

Ungrateful for favors and forgetful of benefits, the Jews return insult for kindness and impious contempt for goodness. They ought to know the yoke of perpetual enslavement because of their guilt. See to it that the perfidious Jews never in the future grow insolent, but that they always suffer publicly the shame of their sin in servile fear.

Pope Gregory IX

Crucifiers of Christ ought to be held in continual subjection. *Pope Innocent III*

It would be licit, according to custom, to hold Jews in perpetual servitude because of their crime.

St. Thomas Aquinas

Let the Gospel be preached to them and, if they remain obstinate, let them be expelled. *Pope Leo VII*

Let their eyes be dim so that they cannot see, and let them walk bent-backed forever with a heavy load.

Psalm 68:24

The Jews wander over the entire earth, their backs bent over and their eyes cast downward, forever calling to our minds the curse they carry with them.

St. Augustine

As wanderers, they must remain upon the earth until their faces are filled with shame and they seek the name of the Lord Jesus Christ. *Pope Innocent III*

Thou shalt eat bread and cover it with the dung that comes out of a man. Thus shall the children of Israel eat their bread all filthy among the nations wither I will cast them out, saith the Lord. *Ezechiel 4:12-13*

The Jews, who killed both the Lord Jesus and the prophets and have persecuted us, do not please God, and they have become adversaries to all men, to fill up their sin always; for the wrath of God has come upon them to the end. *I Thessalonians 2:14-16*

One who dies a Jew will be damned.
St. Vincent Ferrer

Those of the seed of Abraham who live according to the Law of Moses and who do not believe in Christ before death shall not be saved; especially they who curse this very Christ in the synagogues; who curse everything by which they might obtain salvation and escape the vengeance of fire. *St. Justin the Martyr*

Cursed shall you be in the city, cursed in the field. Cursed be your barn and your stores. Cursed shall be the fruit of your womb, the fruit of your ground, the herds of your oxen, and the flocks of your sheep. Cursed shall you be coming in and cursed going out.
Deuteronomy 28:16-19

Jews are cursed and covered with malediction. The curse has penetrated them like water in their bowels and oil in their bones. They are cursed in the city and cursed in the country, cursed in their coming in and cursed in their going out. Cursed are the fruits of their loins, of their lands, of their flocks; cursed are their cellars, their granaries, their shops, their food, the very crumbs off their tables! *St. Agobard*

The most holy Roman Church firmly believes, professes, and teaches that the Mosaic Law cannot be observed without the loss of eternal salvation. Every one, therefore, who observes circumcision and the Sabbath and the other requirements of the Law, the Church declares not in the least fit to participate in eternal salvation.   *Council of Florence*

No man cometh to the Father but by Me.
St. John 14:6

Whosoever denies the Son does not have the Father.
I St. John 2:23

He who honors not the Son, honors not the Father Who sent Him. He who hates Me, hates My Father also.   *St. John 5:23; 15:23*

If any man love not Our Lord Jesus Christ, let him be anathema.   *I Corinthians 16:22*

O Jewish hearts, harder than rocks!   *St. Ambrose*

For all the House of Israel is a hard forehead and an obstinate heart.   *Ezechiel 3:7*

O intelligence coarse, dense, and cow-like, which did not recognize God even in His own works! Perhaps the Jew will complain that I call his intelligence bovine, but his intelligence is *less* than bovine: "The ox knows his Owner, and the ass knows his Master's crib, but Israel has not known Me, and My people have not understood" (Isaias 1:3). You

53

see, O Jew, I am easier on you than your own prophet!   *St. Bernard*

Canon Law forbids all intercourse with Jews.
                              St. Bernardine of Feltre

Indeed, if any one of the clergy or faithful has taken
a meal with Jews, he is to abstain from Communion
so that he may be reformed.   *Council of Elvira*

How dare Christians have the slightest intercourse
with Jews! They are lustful, rapacious, greedy, perfidious bandits: pests of the universe! Their synagogue is a house of prostitution, the domicile of the
devil, as is the soul of the Jew. As a matter of fact,
Jews worship the devil; their religion is a disease,
their synagogue an abyss of perdition. The rejection
and dispersion of the Jews was done by the wrath of
God because of His absolute abandonment of the
Jews. God *hates* the Jews, and on Judgment Day
will say to those who sympathize with them: "Depart
from Me, for you have had intercourse with My
murderers!" Flee, then, from their assemblies, fly
from their houses, and hold their synagogue in hatred and aversion.   *St. John Chrysostom*

Judaism, since Christ, is a corruption; indeed, Judas
is the image of the Jewish people: their understanding of Scripture is carnal; they bear the guilt for
the death of the Savior, for through their fathers
they have killed Christ. The Jews held Him; the Jews
insulted Him; the Jews bound Him; they crowned
Him with thorns; they scourged Him; they hanged
Him upon a tree.   *St. Augustine*

54

Jews are slayers of the Lord, murderers of the prophets, enemies and haters of God, adversaries of grace, enemies of their fathers' faith, advocates of the devil, a brood of vipers, slanderers, scoffers, men of darkened minds, the leaven of Pharisees, a congregation of demons, sinners, wicked men, haters of goodness!   *St. Gregory of Nyssa*

Woe to the sinful nation, a people loaded with iniquity, a wicked seed, ungracious children. They have forsaken the Lord, they have blasphemed the Holy One of Israel, they have gone away backwards. And when you stretch forth your hands, I will turn away My eyes from you, saith the Lord; and when you multiply prayer, I will not hear, for your hands are full of blood.   *Isaias 1:4,15*

And such are the prayers of the Jews, for when they stretch forth their hands in prayer, they only remind God-the-Father of their sin against His Son. And at every stretching-forth of their hands, they only make it obvious that they are stained with the blood of Christ. For they who persevere in their blindness inherit the blood-guilt of their fathers; for they cried out: "His blood be on us *and on our children*" (Mt. 27:25)   *St. Basil the Great*

Poor Jews! You invoked a dreadful curse upon your own heads; and that curse, miserable race, you carry upon you to this day, and to the End of Time you shall endure the chastisement of that innocent blood!
                              St. Alphonsus Maria Liguori

APOSTOLIC DIGEST: BOOK IV

The
BOOK OF
CHRISTIANS

ONLY CATHOLICS CAN BE CHRISTIANS

You are called in one body.
Colossians 3:15

The Church of Christ is one, and must be one. This unity can be realized only by the profession of one faith, by the reception of the same Sacraments, and by an organic adherence to one solitary ecclesiastical authority. ***Pope Paul VI***

It was to the Apostolic College alone, of which Peter is the head, that Our Lord entrusted the one Body of Christ into which all those who belong *in any way* to the People of God *must* be fully incorporated. ***II Vatican Council***

The Church is one, unified, and articulated, after the manner of a physical body. Therefore, whosoever is not joined in the Body is not a member of it and is not in union with Christ its head. ***Pope Pius XI***

Christianity is incarnate in the Catholic Church; it is identified with that perfect and spiritual society that has the Roman Pontiff for its visible head.
Pope Leo XIII

The Church is One, and it is not possible to be both inside and outside what is One. *St. Cyprian*

The Body of the Church is one, not a body made up of a kind of confused mixture of bodies, nor by each of them gathered into an indistinguishable heap or shapeless mass. *St. Hilary of Poitiers*

The Church is visible because she is a Body; therefore, they are straying from divine truth who imagine the Church to be something merely "spiritual" as they say, a Church in which many Christian communities, although separated by faith, could be joined by some kind of bond invisible to the senses. *Pope Pius XII*

He who thinks he can remain a Christian by his own efforts, deserting the institutional bonds of the visible hierarchical Church, is deceiving himself. The fact remains that God established His Church as a bridge over which we *must* pass, leading from our unhappy lot to His salvation. *Pope Paul VI*

Only those are really to be included as members of the Church who have been bapized, and who profess the true faith, and who have not unhappily withdrawn from the Body or, for grave faults, been excluded by legitimate authority. It follows that those who are divided in faith or in government cannot be living in one Body such as this, and cannot be living the life of its one divine Spirit. *Pope Pius XII*

Outside this Body, the Holy Ghost does not give life to anyone. Those outside the Church do not possess the Holy Ghost. The Catholic Church alone is the Body of Christ, and if a man be separated from the Body of Christ he is not one of His members, nor is he fed by His Spirit.   *Pope Paul VI*

If anyone does not have the Spirit of Christ, he does not belong to Christ.   *Romans 8:9*

One cannot love Christ without loving the Church Christ loves. The Spirit of the Church is Christ's own Spirit, and to the extent to which one loves the Church does he possess the Spirit of Christ.
                    Pope John Paul II

Jesus and the Church are indissoluble, inseparable. Christ and the Church are the same *thing*. It is not possible to say "I accept Jesus, but I do not accept the Church."   *Pope John Paul I*

Those who go off to heretics, and all who leave the Church for heresy, abandon the name of Christ. Those who call these men "Christians" are in grievous error, since they neither understand Scripture at all nor the faith which it contains.   *St. Athanasius*

In name only is Christ found among certain heretics who want to be called Christians. In reality, He is no longer among them.   *St. Augustine*

You Protestants! In the entirety of your Reformation you haven't got a Saint whose name you can give your children. You have to borrow your Christian names from the Catholic Church.
                    St. John Mary Vianney

"Christian" is my name, "Catholic" my surname.

St. Pacian

Therefore, let us prove ourselves worthy of that name we have received. For whosoever is called by any other name besides this is not of God.

St. Ignatius of Antioch

He who falls away from the doctrine and faith of the Catholic Church would not be, nor would even be called, a Christian.   *St. Athanasius*

All true Christians are members of the Church.

St. John Eudes

Whosoever and whatsoever he might be, he who is not in Christ's Church is no Christian!   *St. Cyprian*

A manifest heretic is not a Christian, as is clearly taught by St. Cyprian, St. Athanasius, St. Augustine, St. Jerome, and others.   *St. Robert Bellarmine*

No one is entitled to accept a label without its contents.   *Pope Paul VI*

Many will come in My name, saying: "I am Christ," and they will seduce many. Many will say to Me on that day: "Lord, Lord, have we not prophesied in Thy name and cast out devils in Thy name and done many miracles in Thy name?" Then will I profess unto them: Depart from Me, you who work iniquity; I never knew you!   *St. Matthew 24:4-5; 7:21-23*

For they are false apostles, deceitful workers, disguising themselves as apostles of Christ. And no wonder, for Satan himself disguises himself as an angel of light. Therefore, it is no great thing if his ministers disguise themselves as ministers of justice.
II Corinthians 11:13-15

Heretics do not have the same God, the same Christ, as do Catholics.   *Tertullian*

Heretics worship a God who is a liar, and a Christ who is a liar.   *St. Augustine*

In no way can men be counted among the children of God unless they take the Church for their Mother.
Pope Leo XIII

No one is our brother unless he has the same Father we have.   *St. Jerome*

And, just as the Church cannot err in faith and morals; so, on the contrary, all other societies arrogating to themselves the name of "church" must necessarily be sunk in the most pernicious errors, both doctrinal and moral, because they are guided by the devil.   *Catechism of Trent*

How can "two or three gather in Christ's name" if they have obviously cut themselves off from Christ and His Gospel? Do they think Christ is with them in their gatherings when those gatherings are outside the Church of Christ?   *St. Cyprian*

Therefore, neither faith without the Church nor the Church without the faith can save you.

St. Francis de Sales

If anyone says that a justified man, however perfect he might be, is not bound to observe the commandments of God and of the Church, but is bound only to believe, as though the Gospel apart from the observance of the commandments were an unconditional and absolute promise of everlasting life: let him be anathema. *Council of Trent*

The Holy, Catholic, Apostolic, Roman Church is the only true Church of Jesus Christ. It is error to believe that men can find the path of eternal salvation and attain eternal salvation in the practice of any religion whatsoever. It is error to believe that Protestantism is nothing other than a different form of the same true Christian religion, in which it is permitted to please God equally as in the Catholic Church.

Ven. Pope Pius IX

If anyone says that the condition of the faithful and those who have not yet come to the true faith is equal: let him be anathema. *I Vatican Council*

Therefore, let them tremble who imagine that any religion will lead them to the haven of eternal happiness; let them reflect on the words of the Savior Himself: "He who is not with Me is against Me"; that those who gather not with Him scatter; and that consequently, beyond a doubt, they who do not keep the Catholic faith entire and unchanged will perish in eternity. *Pope Gregory XVI*

THOSE WHO REJECT CHRIST'S CHURCH ARE ANTI-CHRISTIAN

He who is not with Me is against Me.
St. Matthew 12:30

Our Lord Jesus Christ, in testifying that those who are not with Him are His adversaries, does not designate any particular form of heresy, but declares that all heretics who do not gather with Him scatter His flock and are His enemies.   ***Pope Leo XIII***

Whosoever has cut himself off from the Church of Rome has become an alien to Christianity.
Pope St. Boniface I

One cannot believe in Christ without believing in the Church, the Body of Christ. Be faithful, then, to your faith without falling into the dangerous illusion of separating Christ from His Church. The fidelity promised to Christ can never be separated from fidelity to the Church: "He who hears you, hears Me"! (Lk.10:16).   ***Pope John Paul II***

We hear people continually claiming to love Christ, but without the Church; to listen to Christ, but not to the Church; to belong to Christ, but outside the Church. The absurdity of this is clearly evident in this phrase of the Gospel: "Anyone who rejects you, rejects Me."   *Pope Paul VI*

Even heretics appear to possess Christ, for none of them denies the name of Christ. Nevertheless, anyone who does not confess *everything* that pertains to Christ does in fact deny Christ.   *St. Ambrose*

Hence, the separated heresies have been torn off like dead branches. Some are at a very great distance from Christ, others are disinherited for some slight matter and have made themselves and their children aliens from Him: they are outside the boundaries but have set *themselves* up outside. They have nothing left of Christ but the name.   *St. Epiphanius*

All the leaders of heretics have gone out of Christ's Church to the synagogue of Satan, and they have passed over all together, disagreeing in their opposition to the faith, but agreeing in their leaving it.
                                                    St. Jerome

Even if heretics were not enemies of the truth, even if we were not warned to avoid them, what sort of action is it to confer with men who themselves profess that they are still seeking for the truth? For, as long as they are still seeking, they have not laid hold on the truth, they have not as yet believed, *they are not Christians*.   *Tertullian*

The Catholic Church alone, then, Christ calls His Spouse. The Church, therefore, is one; this cannot be said amongst any of those who are heretics or schismatics. The churches of every one of the heretics is prostituted; they are churches which Christ repudiates as unnecessary, since He is the Spouse of One Church.   *St. Optatus of Milevis*

The Lord severed the Jewish people from His kingdom, and heretics and schismatics are also severed from the kingdom of God and from the Church. Our Lord makes it perfectly clear that every assembly of heretics and schismatics belongs not to God, but to the unclean spirit.   *St. Ambrose*

"The multitude of believers had only one heart and soul" (Acts 4:32); but dissenters, and those who separate themselves from the Body of the Church, have no participation in this Holy House.
                    St. Hilary of Poitiers

Since they deny the Gospel and contradict the Creed, they cannot celebrate with us. And, although they dare to claim the name of Christ, every creature whose head is Christ scorns them.
                    Pope St. Leo the Great

All these most ridiculous heretics, who wish to be called Christians, try to give a favorable appearance to their wild figments of imagination which the common sense of mankind utterly abhors. *St. Augustine*

TRUE FAITH CAN BE FOUND ONLY IN THE CATHOLIC CHURCH

Outside are dogs, and sorcerers, and the unchaste, and murderers, and servers of idols, and every one who loves and makes a lie.   *Apocalypse 22:15*

Outside the Church full knowledge of Christ cannot be had, since to her and not to others has been entrusted the task of proclaiming His mystery under the guidance of the Holy Spirit to all nations to the end of the world.   ***Pope John Paul II***

The Church alone is the depository of the truth.
Pope St. Pius X

The Catholic Church alone is the source of truth. If any man does not enter it, or if any man departs from it, he is far from the hope of life and salvation.
Lactantius

Innovators say the Lord gives each of the faithful a clear knowledge of Scripture. Behold, the "private interpretation" of the heretics which has produced such a variety of creeds! Hence, everyone knows that among the Reformers there are as many formulas of faith as there are individuals! This alone is sufficient to show they are in error and do not have the true faith. God arranged that the true faith would be preserved in the Roman Church alone so that, there being but one Church, there would be but one faith and one doctrine for all the faithful.

St. Alphonsus Maria Liguori

The Church clearly knows and maintains that there is but one truth, and consequently contrary "truths" cannot exist. *Pope John XXIII*

There is only one Christian faith, that is: Catholic.

St. Bridget of Sweden

Neither the true faith nor eternal salvation is to be found outside the Holy Catholic Church.

Ven. Pope Pius IX

Those who are seeking the true religion will never find it outside the Catholic Church alone, because in every other religion, if they trace it up to the author, they will find some imposter whose imagination furnished a mass of sophisms and errors.

Alphonsus Maria Liguori

Heretics think false things about God and call it their "faith." *St. Augustine*

The sense of Scripture can be found incorrupt *nowhere* outside the Catholic Church. *Pope Leo XIII*

Faith in Christ cannot be maintained pure and unalloyed when it is not protected and supported by faith in the Church. Faith in Christ and in the Church stand together. Whenever a person obstinately separates himself from the infallible teaching of the Church, he gradually loses the certain and true doctrine about Jesus Christ. All heretics wish to dissolve Christ and therefore "are not of God" (I Jn. 4:3). *Pope Pius XI*

The task of interpreting authentically the Word of God has been entrusted *exclusively* to the living teaching office of the Church. *II Vatican Council*

The Gospel message does not permit either indifference, syncretism, or accommodation. It is a question of peoples' salvation! *Pope John Paul II*

The Church is afflicted at present by Indifferentism: that vicious manner of thinking which holds that eternal salvation can be obtained by the profession of any faith, provided a man's morals be good and decent. Let them beware who preach that the gates of Heaven are open to every religion! Without a doubt, they will perish in eternity unless they hold to the Catholic faith and observe it whole and inviolate. *Pope Gregory XVI*

"Jesus, going into one of the ships that belonged to Simon, asked him to draw back a little; and, sitting down, He taught the multitudes out of the Ship" (Lk. 5:3). The Church is the Ship outside which it is impossible to understand the Divine Word. *St. Hilary of Poitiers*

Wherefore, all heretics, because they are blind to the truth, are forced to wander willy-nilly, first in one direction, then in another. *St. Irenaeus of Lyons*

Therefore, none of the heretics holds the truth; the Church alone is in possession of the truth.

St. Ambrose

Hence, because truth must be one, of all the different churches only one can be the true one, and out of that Church there is no salvation. To convince all heretical sects of their error, there is no way more certain than to show that our Catholic Church has been the first one founded by Jesus Christ; for, this being established, it is proven beyond all doubt that ours is the only true Church and that all the others are certainly in error. A single contradiction is enough to show that Calvin and Luther did not have the Spirit of God.   *St. Alphonsus Maria Liguori*

Because there is no Holy Spirit outside the Church, it is impossible for there to be any sound faith not only among heretics but even among those who are established in schism.   *St. Cyprian*

God will have the Paraclete only in those who worship Him in *perfect* faith.   *St. Cyril of Alexandria*

The true faith of the Catholic Church alone is the true source of salvation, from which all heresies, which have only the name of Christ but not the faith of Christ, have been cut off and separated.

St. Epiphanius

And, just as the devil is not Christ, though he tricks people by the name, so likewise a man cannot be taken for a Christian unless he abides in the Gospel of Christ and in the true faith.   *St. Cyprian*

Oh, God! How does it happen that they do not see that, being separated from the Catholic Church and having lost obedience to her, they have also lost the rule of faith, so that they have no sure rule to ascertain what is of the faith or what is not? Thus, they walk in the dark, changing the articles of their belief from day to day.   *St. Alphonsus Maria Liguori*

Heretics are forever making up new creeds, and condemning old ones. They have their annual and monthly faiths, and as many faiths as they have people. They concoct creeds merely to repent of them, and they formulate new ones in order to anathematize those who adhere to their old ones. They all have "Scriptures" in hand, and "Faith" in their mouths, for no purpose but to impose on weak minds.   *St. Hilary of Poitiers*

Thus does Satan manufacture heretics; thus does he weaken the faith. Therefore, do not let a heretic ensnare you just because he can quote a few examples from Scripture. The devil also makes use of texts from Scripture, not to teach but to deceive.
                                    St. Ambrose

Both the devil and his disciples use the testimonies of Holy Scripture, and vehemently indeed. For, they scarcely ever bring forward anything which they do not try to color with the words of Scripture. Read the tracts of such pests, and you will witness a vast heap of Scriptural examples. Hardly a page is not painted with sentences from the Old or New Testaments. But the more secretively they lurk under the shadows of the divine law, the more are they to be avoided; for they are all false apostles, false prophets, and false teachers, and all of them utterly heretics. Thus, what shall Catholic men do to discern truth from falsehood in the Holy Scriptures? Take very great care to interpret the Scriptures according to the traditions of the universal Church. Within this truly Catholic and Apostolic Church, it is necessary to follow *universality, antiquity,* and *agreement.*

St. Vincent of Lerins

Therefore, heretics are not to be admitted to *any* discussion whatsoever concerning Sacred Scripture. Our faith owes obedience to the Apostle when he forbids us to deal with a heretic "after one warning" (Titus 3:10), not after a disputation with him. Heretics rely on what they have falsely composed from some ambiguity of their own. You will gain nothing but frustration from their blasphemy! The only question to be discussed and the first one to be proposed is: to whom does the true faith belong? For, wherever the true Christian faith can be shown, there will be the true Scriptures, the true interpretations of the Scriptures, and all the true Christian traditions.

Tertullian

When a dispute has arisen concerning doctrine, and everyone uses the same Scriptures to support their contentions, what does a good life afford? If, after so many efforts, one falls into heresy and is cut off from the Church, what does an austere life avail him? Nothing! *St. John Chrysostom*

What good can there be in a man, what can one think of his "fear of the Lord" or his "faith," when neither warnings correct him, nor persecutions induce him to reform?   *St. Cyprian*

What is the use of fighting for many articles of faith and to perish for the doubting of a few? He believes no one article of the faith who refuses to believe any single one. However many Catholic dogmas he retains, yet if he perniciously plucks out one, that which he holds, he holds not by orthodox faith, without which it is impossible to please God, but by his own reason, his own conviction.

St. Edmund Campion

It is a denial of the faith not to confess even in the smallest matter. For we ought not, even in the slightest particular, deviate from the way of truth.

St. Epiphanius

Neither living nor lifeless faith remains in a heretic who disbelieves a single article of faith. All those who deny one article of faith, regardless of their reason, are by that very fact excommunicated. Hence, he who does not adhere to *everything* Jesus Christ has prescribed for our salvation does not have any more of the doctrine of Jesus Christ than the pagans, Jews, or Mohammedans.   *St. Thomas Aquinas*

There can be nothing more dangerous for us than those heretics who admit nearly the entire cycle of Catholic doctrine and yet, by a single word, as with a drop of poison, infect the real and simple faith taught by Our Lord and handed down by Apostolic tradition. For, such is the nature of the faith that nothing can be more absurd than to accept some things and to reject others. If, then, it be certain that *anything* is revealed by God, and this is not believed, then *nothing* whatever is believed. He who dissents even in one point from divinely-revealed truth absolutely rejects all faith.　　　　*Pope Leo XIII*

They even debase the concept of true religion and, little by little, lapse into Naturalism and Atheism.
　　　　　　　　　　　　　　　Pope Pius XI

There is no middle way between Catholicism and Atheism; hence, Protestants have abandoned themselves to the extreme of Atheism or Materialism, denying every maxim of the faith. If you take away obedience to the Church, there is *no* error which will not be embraced.　　*St. Alphonsus Maria Liguori*

You deserters rave, steeped as you are in sacrilege; yes, you rave! What madness could be greater? Why are your ears deaf to the rules of salvation we propose? Look at the punishments we see overtaking men who have denied the faith. Alas! What an evil end they come to! Not even here below can they go unpunished, though the Day of Reckoning is still to come!　　　　　　　　　　　*St. Cyprian*

THERE IS NO ALLEGIANCE TO CHRIST WITHOUT SUBMISSION TO THE POPE

He who hears you hears Me; and he who despises you, despises Me.

St. Luke 10:16

Although the devil desired to sift all the disciples, the Lord testifies that He Himself asked for Peter alone, and wished that the others be confirmed by him (Lk. 22:32); and to Peter as well was committed the care of "feeding the sheep" (Jn. 21:15); and also to him did the Lord hand over the "keys to the kingdom of Heaven" (Mt. 16:19). If, however, anyone believes contrary to this, let him know he is condemned and anathematized. Consider, therefore, that whoever has not been in the peace and unity of the Church cannot have the Lord. Those not willing to be at agreement in the Church of God cannot abide with God. For the Church of God is established among those known to preside over the Apostolic Sees, and whoever separates himself from these Sees is manifestly in schism. *Pope Pelagius II*

Remember and understand well that where Peter is, there is the Church; that those who refuse to associate in communion with the Chair of Peter belong to Antichrist, not to Christ. He who would separate himself from the Roman Pontiff has no further bond with Christ.   *Pope Leo XIII*

It is necessary for salvation that all the faithful of Christ be subject to the Roman Pontiff.
                                    V Lateran Council

It is absolutely necessary that the Christian community be subject in all things to the Sovereign Pontiff if it wishes to be a part of the divinely-established society founded by our Redeemer.   *Pope Pius XII*

No one is found in the one Church of Christ, and no one perseveres in it, unless he acknowledges and accepts obediently the supreme authority of St. Peter and his legitimate successors.   *Pope Pius XI*

The Roman Pontiff is the direct and immediate pasor of *every* soul redeemed by Christ, for he is our Redeemer's Vicar.   *I Vatican Council*

It is impossible to be joined to God except through Jesus Christ; it is impossible to be united to Christ except in and through the Church; finally, it is impossible to belong to the Church except through the bishops who are united to the Supreme Pastor, the successor of Peter.   *Pope John XXIII*

If, therefore, the Greeks or others say that they are not committed to Peter and to his successors, they necessarily say that they are not of the sheep of Christ, since the Lord says that there is only *one* fold and *one* shepherd (Jn. 10:16). Whoever, therefore, resists this authority, resists the command of God Himself. ***Pope Boniface VIII***

Christ expressly pointed out which Church He estalished when He turned to Peter and said: "You are Rock, and upon this Rock I will build *My* Church." Yes, "His" Church - the one Church of Christ - not "many" churches. ***St. Maximilian Mary Kolbe***

It is an error to believe that a man is in the Church if he abandons the See of Peter, the foundation of the Church. ***St. Cyprian***

Where Peter is, there is the Church. ***St. Ambrose***

As ye are children of Christ, so be ye children of Rome! ***St. Patrick***

To be Christian, one must be Roman, governed by Christ's Vicar on earth. The Church does not rest on Christ alone, *but also on Peter*. That Christ and His Vicar constitute only one single Head is solemn teaching. Therefore, those who think they can accept Christ as the Head of the Church without adhering faithfully to His Vicar on earth are in dangerous error. ***Pope Pius XII***

CHAPTER FIVE

SACRAMENTS IMPART NO LIFE OUTSIDE THE TRUE CHURCH

*For God doth not give
the Spirit by measure.*
St. John 3:34

The Sacraments, which some people keep and use outside the unity of Christ, are able to preserve the appearance of piety; but the invisible and spiritual virtue of true piety cannot abide there any more than feeling can remain in an amputated part of your body. **Pope Leo XIII**

The Church alone possesses the beneficial use of the Sacraments, the efficacious instruments of grace.
Catechism of Trent

Cut off from the Body into which alone the graces of Christ flow, you are deprived of the benefit of all Sacraments. **St. Edmund Campion**

The Gentiles have churches, and scriptures, and sacrifices, and teachers, and books, and a partial knowledge of God; nevertheless, no one on earth possesses the grace and operation of the Holy Spirit except those who have been rightly baptized by faith in the Father, Son, and Holy Ghost.
Bl. Jerome of Jerusalem

Hold most firmly, and never doubt in the least, that outside the Catholic Church the Sacrament of Baptism cannot be of any profit; nay, just as within the Church salvation is conferred through the Sacrament of Baptism upon those who believe rightly, so too, outside the Catholic Church, ruin is heaped up for those who were baptized by that same Baptism, if they do not return to the Church.   *St. Fulgentius*

There is no salvation outside the Church, and therefore whatever things of the Church are had outside the Church do not avail unto salvation.
St. Augustine

Anyone who receives the Sacrament of Baptism, whether in the Catholic Church or in a heretical or schismatic church, receives the whole Sacrament; however, he will not have salvation if he has that Sacrament outside the Catholic Church. Eternal life can never in any way be obtained by anyone who, with the Sacrament of Baptism, remains a stranger to the Catholic Church. Hold most firmly and never doubt in the least that no person baptized outside the Catholic Church can become a partaker of eternal life if, before the end of this earthly life, he has not returned, and been incorporated into the Catholic Church.   *St. Fulgentius*

Some men can receive Baptism outside the Church, but no one can either receive or possess salvation outside the Church. For the water of the Church is salutary and holy for those who use it well, but outside the Church no one can use it well.
St. Augustine

There are many heresies which utilize the words of Baptism, but not in a proper sense, nor with sound faith; and, in consequence, the water which they pour is unprofitable, so that he who is sprinkled by them is polluted rather than redeemed.

St. Athanasius

Although among heretics and schismatics there is the same Baptism, nevertheless, remission of sins is not operative among them because of the rottenness of discord and wickedness of dissension. *St. Augustine*

Without a doubt, the forgiveness of sins is the work of the Holy Spirit and is granted by God, but not independently of the Church founded by Jesus Christ for the salvation of all men. *Pope John Paul II*

Besides a desire to be baptized, faith is also necessary to obtain the grace of the Sacrament. Our Lord said: "He who *believes* and is baptized shall be saved" (Mk. 16:16). *Catechism of Trent*

Therefore, Baptism without faith avails nothing. If anyone without the right faith receives Baptism outside the Church, he does not receive it unto salvation. Men can receive the Baptism of the Church outside her fold, but no one can receive or keep the salvation of the blessed outside the Church.

St. Thomas Aquinas

Baptism does not profit a man outside unity with the Church, for many heretics also possess this Sacrament, but not the fruits of salvation. Children baptized in other communions cease to be members of the Church when, after reaching the age of reason, they make formal profession of heresy, as, for example, by receiving communion in a non-Catholic church.   *St. Augustine*

They no longer have the Sacraments, with the exception of Baptism; a fruitful baptism for children, provided that, once the age of reason is reached, they do not embrace the schism.   *Pope Leo XIII*

Heretics and schismatics place an obstacle to God's grace by their sins of infidelity and schism in which they actually persevere.   *St. Robert Bellarmine*

The Church is built on the Rock of Peter, and he who eats the Lamb outside this holy dwelling has no part with God.   *Ven. Pope Pius IX*

Outside the unity of faith and love which makes us members of the Church, no one can be saved; hence, if the Sacraments are received outside the Church, they are not effective for salvation even though they be true Sacraments. However, they can become useful if a person returns to Holy Mother the Church, the solitary Spouse of Christ, whose sons alone Christ considers worthy of eternal inheritance.
                              St. Bonaventure

THERE CAN BE NO COMMUNION WITH NON-CATHOLICS

If a man will not hear the Church let him be to thee as the heathen and publican.
St. Matthew 18:17

Some people hope that nations, in spite of their differing religious viewpoints, may unite as brothers in the profession of certain doctrines as a common foundation. Certainly, efforts such as these *cannot* receive the approbation of Catholics, for they rest on the false opinion that any religion whatever is more-or-less praiseworthy and good. Those who hold this opinion are in gross error! Is it permitted for Catholics to be present at conventions, gatherings, meetings, or societies of non-Catholics which aim to associate everyone who in any way lays claim to the name of Christian? *In the negative!* This Apostolic See has *never* allowed its subjects to take part in the assemblies of non-Catholics.   *Pope Pius XI*

Do not work together with unbelievers, for what does justice have in common with injustice?
II Corinthians 6:14

Whoever is separated from the Church must be a-voided and fled from; such a man is a sinner and is self-condemned. *St. Cyprian*

It is an illusion to seek the company of sinners on the pretence of reforming them, or of converting them; it is far more to be feared that they will spread their poison to us. *St. Gregory Nazianzen*

Therefore, it is unlawful, and an act the punishment of which is death, to love to associate with unholy heretics. *St. Cyril of Alexandria*

If you embrace the errors of the nations that dwell among you, and make marriages with them, and join friendships with them, know ye for a certainty that they shall be a pit and a snare in your way, and a stumbling block at your side. *Josue 23:13*

Saints Peter and Paul loathed heretics, and warned us to avoid them. *St. Cyprian*

If any man, who is called a brother, be a server of idols, with such a one do not keep company, *not so much as to eat*. For what fellowship does light have with darkness? Or what part do the faithful have with the unbeliever? Wherefore, go out from among them, and be ye separate, saith the Lord.
Corinthians I, 5:11; II, 6:14-17

Such was the horror which the Apostles and their disciples had against holding even verbal communication with any corrupters of the truth!
St. Irenaeus of Lyons

In respect to their guilt whereby they are opposed to God, *all sinners are to be hated*, even one's father, or mother, or kindred. For it is our duty to hate in the sinner his being a sinner.   *St. Thomas Aquinas*

He who hates not his father and mother, and wife and children, and brothers and sisters cannot be My disciple.   *St. Luke 14:26*

He who loveth father or mother more than Me is not worthy of Me; and he who loveth son or daughter more than Me is not worthy of Me.
                                    St. Matthew 10:37

If any man come to you and bring not this doctrine, do not receive him into the house nor say to him: "God speed you." For, he who says to him "God speed you" communicates with his wicked works.
                                    II St. John 1:10-11

Since these wretched souls will have to be separated from God and Heaven for all eternity because their place will be in Hell, already here on earth they have to be separated from the company of Christ and His servants.   *St. Louis Marie de Montfort*

It is impossible for us to hold communion after their death with those who have not been in communion with us during their life.   *Pope Innocent III*

If any man shall be friendly to those with whom the Roman Pontiff is not in communion, he is in complicity with those who want to destroy the Church of God; and, although he may seem to be with us in body, he is against us in mind and spirit, and is a much more dangerous enemy than those outside.

Pope St. Clement I

I pray to God that, as high as we seem to sit treading heretics under our feet like ants, we live not to see the day we would gladly wish to be at league and composed with them, to let them have their churches quietly to themselves so that they would be content to let us have ours quietly to ourselves.

St. Thomas More

We charge you, brethren, in the name of Our Lord Jesus Christ, that you withdraw from every brother walking disorderly and not according to the tradition received from us. And, if any man does not obey, note that man, and do not keep company with him.

II Thessalonians 3:6,14

If any ecclesiastic or layman shall go into the synagogue of the Jews or to the meeting-houses of the heretics to join in prayer with them, let them be deposed and deprived of communion. If any bishop or priest or deacon shall join in prayer with heretics, let him be suspended.   *III Council of Constantinople*

One must neither pray nor sing psalms with heretics, and whosoever shall communicate with those who are cut off from the communion of the Church, whether clergy or layman: let him be excommunicated.

Council of Carthage

I will not pray with you, nor shall you pray with me; neither will I say "Amen" to your prayers, nor shall you to mine.   *St. Margaret Clitherow*

These men are Protestants; they are heretics! Have nothing to do with them!   *St. Anthony Mary Claret*

Heretics deserve not only to be separated from the Church by excommunication, but also to be severed from the world by death. For it is a much more serious matter to corrupt the faith than to counterfeit that which supports temporal life. Wherefore, if counterfeiters and other evil-doers are immediately condemned to death by secular authorities, there is much more reason for heretics to be put to death.
          St. Thomas Aquinas

Heresy is a kind of treason, and if a heretic persisteth in his false belief, he may be handed over to be burned.   *St. Thomas More*

Even if my own father were a heretic, I would gather the wood to burn him!   *Pope Paul IV*

That it is against the will of the Spirit to burn heretics at the stake is condemned as false. *Pope Leo X*

Make no mistake, my brethren: they who endeavor to corrupt the Church of Christ shall suffer everlasting punishment. Whosoever sets at nought His doctrine shall go into Hell, and so shall everone who listens to him. What communion does light have with darkness, or Christ with Belial? Or what portion does truth have with falsehood? Or righteousness with unrighteousness? Or true doctrine with that which is false? *St. Ignatius of Antioch*

I beseech you, brethren, mark those who made dissensions and offenses contrary to the doctrine which you have learned, and avoid them. *Romans 16:17*

A man who is a heretic, after the first and second admonition, avoid; knowing that such a man is subverted and sins, being condemned by his own judgment. *St. Titus 3:10-11*

Do not treat with a man without religion. Give no heed to them in *any* matter of counsel. *Ecclesiasticus 37:12,14*

I cannot communicate with unclean heretics even by a single word! *St. Paphnutius*

Predestinate souls, you who are of God, cut yourselves adrift from those who are damning themselves! *St. Louis Marie de Montfort*

We have become cowardly, faint-hearted, and, so often, for some reason or another, we keep silence. We let ourselves be overcome by human respect, and cease to show ourselves as true followers of Our Lord. Why? Because we are cowards! Oh, how we need to renew our faith, to rekindle our hearts in the sublime principles of our holy religion! *St. Frances Xavier Cabrini*

APOSTOLIC DIGEST: BOOK V

The
BOOK OF
OBEDIENCE

CHAPTER ONE

THERE IS NO SALVATION WITHOUT PERSONAL SUBMISSION TO THE POPE

I say to thee that thou art Peter; and upon this rock I will build My Church, and the gates of Hell shall not prevail against it.   *St. Matthew 16:18*

No man outside obedience to the Pope of Rome can ultimately be saved. All who have raised themselves against the faith of the Roman Church and died in final impenitence have been damned, and gone down into Hell.   ***Pope Clement VI***

It is an absolute necessity to submit to the Supreme Pastor, to whom it is absolutely necessary for salvation to remain subject.   ***Pope Leo XIII***

We declare, say, define, and pronounce that it is absolutely necessary for the salvation of every human creature to be subject to the Roman Pontiff.
          Pope Boniface VIII

Blessed Peter received the keys of the kingdom in such a way that all may understand that whosoever shall cut themselves off in any way cannot enter the kingdom of Heaven. Peter is the doorkeeper whom I will not contradict lest, when I come to the gates of

Heaven, there should be no one to open them, since he will be my adversary who is proven to have the keys.   *St. Bede the Venerable*

Christ Jesus left you this sweet key of obedience; for He left His Vicar, whom you are all obliged to obey until death. And whoever is outside his obedience is in a state of damnation.   *St. Catherine of Siena*

I am moved to obedience to that See by this fact especially: that, on the one hand, every enemy of the Christian faith makes war on that See; and, on the other, no one has ever declared himself an enemy of that See who has not also, shortly afterward, shown that he was the enemy of the Christian religion.
                              St. Thomas More

He who does not enter by the door of the fold shall not have salvation. The door of the fold is the Catholic Church and union with the Head who represents Jesus Christ.   *St. Frances Xavier Cabrini*

How beautiful is the Church of Christ, "the fold of the sheep"! Into this fold of Jesus Christ no man may enter unless he be led by the Sovereign Pontiff, and only if they be united to him can men be saved.
                              Pope John XXIII

To be subject to the Roman Pontiff is absolutely necessary for salvation.   *St. Thomas Aquinas*

You may no more refuse obedience to the See of Rome than might a child refuse obedience to his natural father. That is my opinion; that is the belief in which, by the grace of God, I shall die.

St. Thomas More

Those who are obstinate toward the authority of the Roman Pontiff cannot obtain eternal salvation.

Ven. Pope Pius IX

We teach and declare that this power of jurisdiction of the Roman Pontiff is immediate, to which everyone, both pastors and faithful, are bound to submit.

I Vatican Council

It is error to believe that, if the Pope were a reprobate and an evil man and consequently a member of the devil, he has no power over the faithful.

Council of Constance

It is error to believe that, if the Pope were wicked and reprobate, then he is of the devil and is not head of the Church Militant since he would not be a member of it.

Pope Martin V

Even if the Pope were Satan incarnate, we ought not to raise up our heads against him, but calmly lie down to rest on his bosom. He who rebels against our Father is condemned to death, for that which we do to him we do to Christ: we honor Christ if we honor the Pope; we dishonor Christ if we dishonor the Pope. I know very well that many defend themselves by boasting: "They are so corrupt, and work all manner of evil!" But God has commanded that, even if the priests, the pastors, and Christ-on-earth were incarnate devils, we be obedient and subject to them, not for their sakes, but for the sake of God, and out of obedience to Him.

St. Catherine of Siena

All Catholics agree that it is possible for the Pope, even as Pope with an Ecumenical Council, to err in controversies of fact which depend on human testimony; secondly, that it is possible for him, even in universal questions of faith or morals, to err as a private teacher from ignorance, which happens to other teachers. Next, all Catholics agree that the Pope, with an Ecumenical Council, cannot err in framing decrees of faith or morality; secondly, that the Pope, when determining anything in a doubtful matter, whether by himself or with his own particular Council, whether it be possible for him to err or not, is to be obeyed by all the faithful. *St. Robert Bellarmine*

If anyone condemns the dogmas or decrees promulgated for the Catholic faith and the correction of the faithful by the one presiding in the Apostolic See, let him be anathema. *Pope St. Nicholas the Great*

It would be possible to multiply indefinitely citations from the best witnesses, all of whom clearly declare the attachment, veneration, submission, and obedience which must be accorded the Apostolic See and the Roman Pontiff by those who wish to belong to the one, true, holy Church of Christ in order to obtain eternal salvation. *Ven. Pope Pius IX*

NO ONE CAN BE SAVED WHO REFUSES OBEDIENCE TO THE PASTORS OF THE CHURCH

He who will be proud and refuse to obey the commandment of the priest, that man shall die.   *Deuteronomy 17:12*

Just as no man can enter any place without the help of him who has the keys, so no one is admitted to Heaven unless its gates be unlocked by the priests to whose custody the Lord gave the keys.

Catechism of Trent

Look at the heathens. What has it availed them that Our Lord has died? Alas! They can have no share in the blessing of redemption while they have no priests to apply His blood to their souls!

St. John Mary Vianney

Without priests, we cannot be saved.

St. John Chrysostom

We ought to keep our minds ready to obey in all things our Holy Mother, the hierarchical Church. We ought always believe that what seems to us *white* to be *black* if the hierarchical Church so defines it. I ought to be like a corpse, which does not have either free will or understanding; or like a staff in the hands of an old man who uses it as may please him. *St. Ignatius Loyola*

With all thy soul, fear the Lord, and reverence His priests. Forsake not His ministers, and give honor to the priests. *Ecclesiasticus 7:31-33*

Do not let those who have refused to obey the bishops and priests imagine that the way of salvation is still open to them. Heresies and schisms all have their origin solely in the refusal to obey the priest of God. *St. Cyprian*

Obey your prelates, and be subject to them! *Hebrews 13:17*

It is impossible to be joined to God except through Jesus Christ; it is impossible to be united to Christ except in and through the Church; finally, it is impossible to belong to the Church except through the bishops who are successors of the Apostles united to the Supreme Pastor, the successor of Peter. *Pope John XXIII*

The people united to the priest, and the flock cleaving to the shepherd: this is the Church. The bishop is in the Church and the Church is in the bishop; so that, if a man be not with the bishop, he is not in the Church. *St. Cyprian*

There is no knowledge of God in the land, for people are like those who contradict the priest. *Osee 4:1,4*

After God, the priest. That sums up everything. Leave a parish twenty years without a priest, and they will be worshipping the animals.

St. John Mary Vianney

Does a man think he is with Christ when he acts in opposition to the bishops of Christ and cuts himself off from the society of His clergy and people? An enemy of the altar, he gives up faith for perfidy, religion for sacrilege; an undutiful son, despising the bishops and deserting the priests of God, he tries to set up a new altar. *St. Cyprian*

It is impossible for another altar to be set up, or a new priesthood to be established, apart from the one altar and the one priesthood. *Pope John XXIII*

Therefore, follow the bishops and priests. Apart from them, there is nothing that can be called a church. Anyone outside is impure; he is worse than an infidel. In other words, anyone who acts apart from the bishop and the priests and deacons does not have a clean conscience. For, all who belong to God and to Jesus Christ are with the bishop. Make no mistake about it: no one who follows another into schism inherits the kingdom of God.

St. Ignatius of Antioch

THE SACRAMENTS ADMINISTERED BY PRIESTS ARE NECESSARY FOR THE SALVATION OF ALL MANKIND

They brought to Him everyone who was diseased, and as many as touched were made whole. *St. Matthew 14:35-36*

Our most merciful Lord has bequeathed to His Church the Sacraments through which we firmly believe that the fruit of His passion is really communicated to us. For through the Sacraments, as through a channel, must flow the efficacy of the passion of Christ, that is, the grace He merited for us, without which we cannot hope for salvation.

Catechism of Trent

Sinners are lost not because there was no atonement for their sins, but because they refused to make use of the Sacraments and thus share in the atonement offered by Jesus Christ. ***Bl. John of Avila***

You must submit yourself faithfully to those who have charge of divine things, and you must look to them for the means of your salvation.

Pope St. Gelasius I

All true justification either begins through the Sacraments or, once begun, increases through them, or, when lost, is regained through them.

Council of Trent

Only through receiving the Sacraments of Christ can we come to share in the lot of the Elect and in eternal life. *St. Bede the Venerable*

If anyone says that the Sacraments of the New Law are not necessary for salvation, but that they are superfluous: let him be anathema. *Council of Trent*

My children, why are there no Sacraments in other religions? *Because there is no salvation there.* We have the Sacraments at our disposal because we belong to the religion of salvation. Give thanks to God for them, for the Sacraments are the sources of salvation. It is not so in other religions.

St. John Mary Vianney

Sins can be forgiven only through the Sacraments when duly administered; hence, it follows that both priests and Sacraments are the instruments which Christ makes use of to accomplish in us the pardon of sin and the grace of justification.

Catechism of Trent

Through priests, God communicates His grace to the faithful in the Sacraments. In a word, without priests, we cannot be saved!

St. Alphonsus Maria Liguori

BAPTISM IS THE UNIVERSAL REQUIREMENT FOR HEAVEN

Unless one be born again of water and the Holy Ghost, he cannot enter into the kingdom of God. *St. John 3:5*

Holy Baptism holds the first place among all the Sacraments because, by it, we are made members of Christ and of His Body, the Church. And since death has come to all men through the first man, unless we are re-born of water and the Holy Ghost, we cannot enter into the kingdom of Heaven.

Council of Florence

Since by the transgression of the first man the whole progeny of the human race is vitiated, no one can be freed from the condition of the old man except by the Sacrament of the Baptism of Christ.

Pope St. Leo the Great

The universal and absolute necessity of Baptism our Savior has declared in these words: "Unless a person be born again of water and the Holy Ghost, he cannot enter into the kingdom of God."

Catechism of Trent

Baptism is the Sacrament of *absolute* necessity. Consequently, it is clear that everyone is bound to be baptized, and that without Baptism there is no salvation for men. *St. Thomas Aquinas*

If anyone says that Baptism is optional, that is, not necessary for salvation: let him be anathema.

Council of Trent

No one ascends into the kingdom of Heaven except by the Sacrament of Baptism. No one is excused from Baptism: not infants, nor anyone hindered by any necessity. When the Lord Jesus came to John, and John said: "I ought to be baptized by Thee, and dost Thou come to me?" Jesus said: "Permit it to be so for now. For thus it becometh us to fulfill all justice" (Mt. 3:14-15). Behold how all justice rests on Baptism! *St. Ambrose*

On account of this rule of faith, even infants are truly baptized unto the remission of sins. Moreover, if anyone says that in the kingdom of Heaven there will be some place where infants live who departed this life without Baptism, without which they cannot enter into the kingdom of Heaven which is eternal life: let him be anathema. *Pope St. Zosimus*

The Lord has determined that the kingdom of Heaven be conferred only on baptized persons. If eternal life can accrue only to those who have been baptized, it follows that they who die unbaptized incur everlasting death. *St. Augustine*

Whether a man departs this life without Baptism, or receives a baptism lacking in some requirements, his loss is the same. *St. Basil the Great*

98

The punishment of being deprived of God and the loss of heavenly glory affects both adults and children who are unbaptized. The children are punished along with the others, but by the mildest punishment because they deserve the Punishment of Loss alone, not the Punishment of the Senses. *St. Bonaventure*

Weep for the unbelievers! Weep for those who differ not a smidgen from the infidels: those who die without Baptism! They are outside the Royal City, along with those subject to punishment, along with the damned. *St. John Chrysostom*

Baptism is the distinctive mark of all Christians, and serves to differentiate them from those who have not been cleansed in this purifying stream and who, consequently, are not members of Christ.

Pope Pius XII

Our heretics, more audacious than Pelagians, deny that Baptism is necessary, not only for the remission of sin, but also for the attainment of Heaven. However, those who imagine that there is another remedy besides Baptism openly contradict the Gospel, the Councils, the Fathers, and the consensus of the universal Church. *St. Robert Bellarmine*

PENANCE IS INDISPENSABLE FOR THE REMISSION OF SIN

Unless you do penance, you shall all likewise perish.   St. Luke 13:5

This Sacrament of Penance is necessary for salvation for those who have fallen after Baptism, just as Baptism itself is necessary for salvation for those not yet regenerated.   ***Council of Trent***

This Sacrament is, after Baptism, indispensably necessary for all who have committed sins who wish to be reconciled to God and enter Heaven. Penance is the only means instituted by Jesus Christ for this; He will never grant remission of sins to Christians who wish to obtain it by some other means. No power in Heaven or on earth can obtain forgiveness of sin but this holy Sacrament.   ***St. John Neumann***

Mortal sins must be confessed not only to God, but also to the priest who has the power to forgive them.   ***St. Robert Bellarmine***

Consider that, unless you confess your sin, you will go to Hell. All mortal sins are to be submitted to the keys of the Church; recourse to these keys is the *only*, the *necessary*, and the *certain* way to forgiveness. Unless those who are guilty of grievous sin have recourse to the power of the keys, they cannot hope for eternal salvation.   *St. Augustine*

The sinner is not restored to the Church except by the decree of the priest. If anyone has Perfect Contrition before the absolution of the priest, he obtains remission of his sins by the fact that he intends to subject himself to the keys of the Church, without which intention there is no real contrition.

St. Thomas Aquinas

Although it does sometimes happen that contrition is made perfect through charity and reconciles a man to God before this Sacrament is actually received, nevertheless, this holy Council teaches that the reconciliation must not be attributed to contrition exclusive of the desire for the Sacrament included in the contrition. If anyone says that the man who falls after Baptism can recover justice by faith alone without the Sacrament of Penance, let him be anathema. If anyone says that, to obtain remission of sins in the Sacrament, it is not necessary according to divine law to confess each and every mortal sin that is remembered, let him be anathema.   *Council of Trent*

Confess your sins, that you may be saved.

St. James 5:16

It is necessary for salvation to confess all mortal sins perfectly and distinctly to the priest.

Pope Clement VI

The necessity of Confession has been commanded by several Councils: III Carthage, Challon, Worms, the Council of the Lateran under Innocent III, by Constance, Florence, and Trent.

St. Alphonsus Maria Liguori

If anyone should depart this life without penance or confession, he is not to be prayed for.

Council of Chalcuth

That, if a man be duly contrite, every exterior confession on his part is superfluous and useless is hereby condemned as error. *Pope Martin V*

In addition to contrition of heart, Christ obligated us out of necessity for salvation to confess to a priest.

Council of Constance

It is impossible for a sinner to be saved unless he confesses his sins to a priest.

Pope St. Leo the Great

That mortal sins are abolished without Confession by means of contrition of heart alone, we declare to be false and entirely at variance with the Gospels.

Pope Sixtus IV

If you do not confess your sins, you will certainly be damned. *St. Alphonsus Maria Liguori*

CHAPTER SIX

THE HOLY EUCHARIST IS
ESSENTIAL TO ETERNAL LIFE

Unless you eat the flesh of the Son of Man and drink His blood, you shall not have life in you.   St. John 6:54

The Eucharist is necessary to preserve the soul in grace, because the soul becomes gradually exhausted if care is not taken to repair its strength. "He who eats My flesh and drinks My blood has everlasting life" (Jn. 6:55). Therefore, he who does not eat this Bread and drink this Blood does not have this Life. Without it, a man may have temporal life, but in no way can he possess eternal life.
                    St. John Baptist de la Salle

Our God has given Himself to be our Food because man, condemned to death as he is, can be restored to Life only by this means.   **Pope Urban IV**

Unless a believer partakes of the Body and Blood of Christ our God, it is impossible to be saved and obtain the kingdom of Heaven.   **St. Nilus**

What would become of us if we did not have the Most Holy Sacrament?   **St. Denis the Areopagite**

Without Jesus, first bloodily sacrificed for us upon the cross, and daily since then unbloodily sacrificed upon our altars, it would all be over for us. Each person might say to the other: "We part to meet in Hell." Yes, in *Hell!*   *St. Leonard of Port Maurice*

One cannot live without the Mass.
Pope John Paul II

God instituted this mystery, without which there would be no salvation in this world.
St. Udone of Cluny

Who but a raving mad lunatic, completely out of his mind, could despise this tremendous mystery?
St. John Chrysostom

Without Baptism and the Lord's Supper, it is impossible for man to attain to salvation and everlasting life. So much does Scripture also testify.
St. Augustine

He gives everyone the same invitation to receive Him: "Take and eat: this is My Body." And, to allure us to receive Him, He promises Heaven to us: "If any man eat of this Bread, he shall live forever." And, if we refuse to receive Him, He threatens us with death: "Unless you eat the flesh of the Son of Man, and drink His blood, you shall not have life in you."   *St. Alphonsus Maria Liguori*

The
BOOK OF
SENTIMENTAL
EXCUSES

CHAPTER ONE

NEITHER BAPTISM OF DESIRE NOR BAPTISM OF BLOOD SUFFICES FOR SALVATION

One Lord, one Faith, one Baptism.
Ephesians 4:5

All the faithful must confess only one Baptism, which regenerates in Christ all the baptized, just as there is one God and one faith. We believe that this Sacrament, celebrated in water, is necessary for children and grown-ups alike for the perfect remedy of salvation. ***Council of Vienne***

Let us hold firmly to our Catholic doctrine: *one* God, *one* faith, *one* Baptism. To try and inquire further is sinful. ***Ven. Pope Pius IX***

We confess one Baptism for the remission of sins. ***The Nicene Creed***

One is the Baptism which the Church administers, of water and the Holy Ghost, with which catechumens need to be baptized. Nor does the mystery of regeneration exist *at all* without water. Now, even the catechumen believes; but, unless he be baptized, he can not receive remission of his sins. ***St. Ambrose***

It is not enough merely to believe. He who believes and is not yet baptized, but is only a catechumen, has not yet fully acquired salvation.

St. Thomas Aquinas

How many sincere catechumens die unbaptized, and are thus lost forever! When we come into the sight of God, no one will say: "Why was this man led by God's direction to be baptized, while that man, although he lived properly as a catechumen, was killed in a sudden disaster and not baptized?" Look for rewards, and you will find nothing but punishments! Of what use would repentance be, if Baptism did not follow? No matter what progress a catechumen may make, he still carries the burden of iniquity, and it is not taken away until he has been baptized.

St. Augustine

You are outside Paradise, O catechumen! You share the exile of Adam! *St. Gregory of Nyssa*

It is obvious that we must grieve for our own catechumens should they depart this life without the saving grace of Baptism. *St. John Chrysostom*

Neither commemoration nor chanting is to be employed for catechumens who have died without Baptism. *Council of Braga*

Consequently, if anyone were sanctified in the womb now, they would need to be baptized in order to be conformed to the other members of Christ by receiving the Character of Baptism. *St. Thomas Aquinas*

But how can you put on Christ unless you receive the Mark of Christ? Unless you receive His Baptism? *St. Gregory of Nyssa*

For it is through Baptism we are made members of Christ and compacted into the Body of the Church. *Pope Eugene IV*

All the multitude of the faithful are regenerated from water and the Holy Spirit, and through this truly incorporated into the Church. *III Council of Valence*

God provides Baptism for *all* His Elect. *St. Robert Bellarmine*

Baptism has been made accessible to everyone, everywhere. *St. Bernard*

Seek first the kingdom of God and His justice, and unto this *all else* will be added. *St. Matthew 6:33*

"All." "All." And He who says "all" excludes *nothing*. *St. Alphonsus Maria Liguori*

Never has anyone who entrusted himself to Our Lord been disappointed or defrauded of his expectations! *St. John Eudes*

God never leaves unrewarded the ardent desires of holy souls. *Bl. Henry Suso*

For God does not forsake those who have once been justified by His grace, unless He first be forsaken by them. *St. Augustine*

Of those who fail to be baptized, some are utterly animal or bestial; others honor Baptism but they delay, some out of carelessness, some because of insatiable passion. Still others are not able to receive Baptism because of infancy or some involuntary circumstance which prevents their receiving the gift, even if they desire it. I think the first group will have to suffer punishment, not only for their other sins, but also for their contempt of Baptism. The second group will also be punished, but less, because it was not through wickedness so much as foolishness that brought about their failure. The third group will be neither glorified, nor punished; for, although un-Sealed, they are not wicked. If you were able to judge a man who intends to commit murder solely by his *intention* and without any *act* of murder, then you could likewise reckon as baptized one who *desired* Baptism, without having *received* Baptism. But, since you cannot do the former, how can you do the latter? Put it this way: if *desire* has equal power with *actual* Baptism, you would then be satisfied to desire Glory, as though that longing itself were Glory! Do you suffer by not attaining the *actual* Glory, so long as you have a *desire* for it? *I cannot see it!*   *St. Gregory Nazianzen*

Shall we void the Gospel? Shall we void the words of Christ? Shall we promise you what He refuses you?   *St. Augustine*

Furthermore, St. Augustine says that Cornelius the Centurion, although praised in the Scriptures, was not yet such that he could have been saved unless he became incorporated in the Church through the Sacrament of Baptism. *St. Robert Bellarmine*

Cornelius and the Good Thief were justified without having any knowledge of Baptism, but everyone knows that the obligation of Baptism did not commence until after the death of the Savior.
St. Alphonsus Maria Liguori

The time when the law of Baptism was made admits of no doubt. After the Resurrection of Our Lord, when He gave to His Apostles the command to go and "teach all nations, baptizing them in the name of the Father, and of the Son, and of the Holy Ghost," the law of Baptism became obligatory on all who were to be saved. *Catechism of Trent*

Baptism is the necessary condition for salvation.
Pope John Paul II

In Baptism, two things are always necessarily required: the words and the element. You ought not doubt that they do not have true Baptism in which one of them is missing. *Pope Innocent III*

In the days of Noah, when the Ark was under construction, eight souls were saved by water; whereunto Baptism, *being of like form*, now saves you also.
I St. Peter 3:20-21

Had Israel not crossed the Sea, they would not have escaped from Pharoah; likewise, if you do not go through the water, you will not escape from the cruel tyranny of the demon. *St. Basil the Great*

If I wash thee not, thou shalt have no part with Me.

St. John 13:8

Some among the heretics flatter themselves with claims of martyrdom. But not all who submit their bodies to suffering, even to flames, are to be considered as having shed their blood for their sheep; rather, they may have shed it *against* the salvation of their sheep, for the Apostle says: "If I should deliver my body to be burned, and have not charity, it profits me *nothing*" (I Corinthians 13:3). Indeed, as long as you remain outside the Church, and severed from the fabric of unity and bond of charity, you will be punished with everlasting chastisement, even if you were burned alive for the sake of Christ.

St. Augustine

Being placed outside the Church, and cut off from unity and charity, Heretics or schismatics could not be crowned in death, even though one should be slain for the name of Christ. Even if a man should deliver his body to be burned, he gains nothing. Baptism of blood cannot profit a heretic unto salvation, because there is no salvation outside the Church. *St. Cyprian*

Outside the Church, no one can be a martyr.

St. Pacian

We should not forget that the devil has his martyrs, and that he infuses into them a false constancy. It is not the punishment, but the cause, that makes the martyr, that is: the true faith.

St. Alphonsus Maria Liguori

If those unwilling to be at agreement in the Church be slain outside the Church, they cannot attain to the rewards of the Church. *Pope Pelagius II*

No one, even if he pour out his blood for the name of Christ, can be saved unless he remain within the bosom and unity of the Catholic Church.
Pope Eugene IV

Nay, though they should suffer death for the Name, the guilt of such men is not removed even by their blood, for not even blood can wash away the stain of heresy. Baptism of fire does not help such a person if he dies outside the Church, for the grievous sin of schism is not purged away even by martyrdom. No martyr can he be who is not in the Church. Such a man may be put to death; crowned he cannot be.
St. Cyprian

When the Lord says: "Unless one be born again of water and the Holy Ghost, he shall not enter into the kingdom of God" (Jn. 3:5), what Catholic will doubt that whoever has not deserved to be a co-heir with Christ will be a partner with the devil?
Pope St. Zosimus

GOD MAKES NO LAW
IMPOSSIBLE TO KEEP

*If you choose, you can keep
the commandments.*
Ecclesiasticus 15:15

If anyone says that the commandments of God are impossible to observe, even for a man who is justified and in the state of grace, let him be anathema.
Council of Trent

All things are possible to him who believes. For, all things are possible with God. *St. Mark 9:22; 10:27*

To him who seeks only to please God and save his soul, the necessities will *never* be lacking.
St. John Mary Vianney

We cannot believe that God would have imposed on us the observance of a law, and then made the law impossible to observe!
St. Alphonsus Maria Liguori

God does not command impossibilities. When God lays a command on you, He requires you to do all you can and, in what you cannot do, to implore His help and He will enable you to do it. He Who com-

113

mands us to do these things grants us aid to ask, to
seek, to knock.   *St. Augustine*

For everyone who asks, receives; and he who seeks,
finds; and to him who knocks, it shall be opened.
                                        St. Matthew 7:8

No one, however much justified, should consider
himself exempt from the observance of the commandments; no one should use that rash statement,
forbidden under anathema, that the observance of
the commandments of God is impossible for one
who is justified. For God does not command impossibilities; on the contrary, He admonishes you to do
what you can, and to pray for what you cannot do,
and He helps you so that you may be able.
                                        Council of Trent

God works that we may both will and do what He
wishes, nor does He allow those gifts to lie idle in us
which He has given us.   *Council of Ephesus*

For, it is God Who works in you both the will and
the performance.   *Philippians 2:13*

Since God commands everyone actually to observe
the commandments, it must certainly be supposed
that He ordinarily gives to everyone at least the re-
mote grace with which, at least by prayer, they can
actually fulfill the Law. Everyone has from God sufficient grace *actually* to fulfill the Law.
                              St. Alphonsus Maria Liguori

SPECULATION IN MATTERS OF FAITH IS PROHIBITED

I cannot go beyond the word of the Lord my God, to utter anything out of my own head, either good or evil.

Numbers 24:13

Extraordinary opinions, even of Catholic Doctors, should not be proposed; instead, the flock should listen to those opinions which have the most certain criteria of Catholic truth: universality, antiquity, and unanimity.   *Pope Clement XIII*

The Church has never accepted as the principal source of truth even the most holy and eminent Doctor. Certainly, the Church considers Augustine and Thomas great Doctors, and she accords them the highest praise; but she recognizes infallibility only in the inspired authors of the Sacred Scriptures. The Church alone is the entrance to salvation and depository of the Sacred Tradition living within her. She alone is the source of truth.   *Pope Pius XII*

Whence, all true Catholics know they ought to receive Doctors, but not to forsake the faith of the Church with Doctors! If at any time any ecclesiastical teacher, yea even a prophet, should attempt to introduce anything new, Divine Providence permits it for our testing. The error of a master is the test of a people; and the greater the education of him who made the error, the greater the test. Such being the case, he is a true and genuine Catholic who places nothing else ahead of the Catholic faith, neither the authority, the genius, the eloquence, nor philosophy of any man whatsoever, but is determined to hold and believe only those things whatsoever he knows the Catholic Church has held universally and from ancient times. But whatsoever he shall perceive to have been introduced later by some one certain man, that which is new and unheard-of, that which is contrary to all the saints, let him know that it does not pertain to religion but rather to temptation.

St. Vincent of Lerins

Caution must be used when there is a question of theories in which the doctrine contained in Sacred Scripture or Tradition is involved. If such conjectural opinions are directly *or indirectly* opposed to the doctrine revealed by God, then the demand that they be recognized can in no way be admitted.

Pope Pius XII

That a scholar is not to be censured if he constructs premises from which it follows that dogmas are false or doubtful, if he does not *directly* deny the dogmas themselves, is condemned as error. *Pope St. Pius X*

The faithful custody of the Deposit of Faith involves the duty to defend the Word of God against whatever would compromise its purity and integrity.

Pope John Paul II

Faith is not to be argued over. Either you accept it with your eyes closed, admitting the inadequacy of the human mind to understand its mysteries, or you reject it. There is no middle way.   *Padre Pio*

Argument may be good for strengthening the intellect, but it is not the true foundation for faith. Faith must be held from obedience, because Christ has commanded it, and Holy Mother the Church ordained it.   *St. Vincent Ferrer*

We ought not to draw distinctions or doubt what is said by the Lord, but be fully convinced that every word of God is true and possible, even though nature fights against it.   *St. Basil the Great*

We ought always hold that what seems to us *white* is *black* if the Church so defines it.
St. Ignatius of Loyola

He who adopts an opinion against a formal text of Scripture, or against the universal sentiment of the Church, cannot be excused from culpable error.
St. Thomas Aquinas

Once it is established that God has revealed a truth, the answer is *Yes* for every one in every age; a *Yes* with conviction and courage, without doubts or hesitations.   *Pope John Paul I*

He who is gifted with the faith is free from inquisitive curiosity; for, when God commands us to believe, He does not propose that we search into His divine judgments nor inquire into their reason and cause, but demands an unchangeable faith. How rash and foolish are they who demand reasons for His saving doctrines! The faith must exclude not only all doubt, but also all desire for demonstration.

Catechism of Trent

For I do not seek to understand in order to believe; rather, I believe in order to understand. *St. Anselm*

Satan knows a lot more theology than any of us, and it does him no good! *St. Maximilian Mary Kolbe*

If the reason for God's Providence is incomprehensible to us, we should not therefore say that there *is* no Providence! *St. Gregory of Nyssa*

God cannot do that which is against the faith. He cannot do what is against truth. *St. Ambrose*

He cannot deny Himself. *II St. Timothy 2:13*

Since truth never contradicts truth, we declare every assertion contrary to the truth of faith to be altogether false; and we strictly decree that all who adhere to errors of this kind are to be shunned and punished as detestable and abominable infidels who disseminate damnable heresies and weaken the Catholic faith.

V Lateran Council

CHAPTER FOUR

THE DOGMAS OF FAITH ADMIT NO ALTERATION WHATSOEVER

Nothing may be taken away, or added.
Ecclesiasticus 18:5

Nothing ever changes in the eternal Catholic doctrine. ***Pope John Paul II***

Nothing can ever pass away from the words of Jesus Christ, nor can anything be changed which the Catholic Church received from Christ to guard, protect, and preach. ***Ven. Pope Pius IX***

The Catholic Faith is such that nothing can be added to it, nothing taken away. Either it is held in its entirety, or rejected totally. This is the Catholic faith, which, unless a man believes faithfully and firmly, he cannot be saved. ***Pope Benedict XV***

And I hold this faith, not as that which seems better and more suited to the culture of a certain age, but in such a way that nothing else is to be believed than by the *words;* and I hold that this absolute and unchangeable truth, which was preached by the Apostles from the earliest times, is to be understood in no way other than by the *words.*
Oath Against Modernism

Add nothing to His words, lest you be reproved and found a liar. ***Proverbs 30:6***

God's Word is one and the same and endures forever unchanged, always the same. ***St. Athanasius***

Wherefore, if there be revealed to us anything new or different, we must in no way give consent to it, not even though it were spoken by an angel.
St. John of the Cross

But though we, or an angel from Heaven, preach a Gospel to you besides that which we have preached to you, let him be anathema! ***Galatians 1:8***

All novelty in faith is a sure mark of heresy. St. Paul cried out aloud, again and again, to all men, to all times, and to all places that, if anyone announces a new dogma, let him be anathematized!
St. Vincent of Lerins

The faith shall never vary in any age, for one is the faith which justifies the Just of all ages. It is unlawful to differ even by a single word from apostolic doctrine. ***Pope St. Leo the Great***

Nothing new is to be allowed, for nothing can be added to the old. Look for the faith of the elders, and do not let our faith be disturbed by a mixture of new doctrines. ***Pope St. Sixtus III***

Our faith is identical with that of the ancients. Deny this, and you dissolve the unity of the Church. We must hold this for certain: that the faith of the people at the present day is one with the faith of the people of past centuries. Were this not true, then we would be in a different church than they and, literally, the Church would not be One. *St. Thomas Aquinas*

I accept the doctrine of faith as handed down to us from the Apostles by the orthodox Fathers, always in the same sense and with the same interpretation.
Pope St. Pius X

For it is not allowable for anyone to change even one word nor allow one syllable to be passed over, mindful of the saying: "Pass not beyond the ancient bounds which thy Fathers have set" (Proverbs 22: 28). *St. Cyril of Alexandria*

The Church has a duty to proclaim the faith without any whittling-down, just as Christ revealed it, and no consideration of time or circumstance can lessen the strictness of this obligation. *Pope Pius XII*

Wretches tainted with Indifferentism and Modernism hold that dogmatic truth is not absolute, but relative; that is, that it must adapt itself to the varying necessities of the times and varying dispositions of souls, since it is not contained in an unchangeable revelation but is, by its very nature, meant to accommodate itself to the life of man. *Pope Pius XI*

Let nothing of the truths that have been defined be lessened, nothing altered, nothing added; but let them be preserved intact in word and in meaning.
Pope Gregory XVI

The faith which God has revealed has not been proposed like a theory of philosophy, to be elaborated upon by human understanding, but as a divine deposit to be faithfully guarded and infallibly declared. Therefore, that sense of sacred dogmas is to be kept forever which Holy Mother Church has once declared, and it must never be deviated from on the specious pretext of a more profound understanding. Let intelligence, and science, and wisdom increase, but only according to the same dogma, the same sense, the same meaning. If anyone shall have said that there may ever be attributed to the doctrines proposed by the Church a sense which is different from the sense which the Church has once understood and now understands: let him be anathema.

I Vatican Council

Under no circumstances can we conceive of the possibility of change, of evolution, or of any modification in matters of faith. The Creed remains always the same.   *Pope Paul VI*

The proposition, that the Apostles' Creed did not have the same meaning for the Christians of the earliest times as for our time, is hereby condemned as erroneous.   *Pope St. Pius X*

Christ's commandment to hear the Church is binding on *all* men, in *every* period, and in *every* country.

Pope Pius XI

What I say to you, I say to *all*.   *St. Mark 13:37*

Therefore, it is necessary to receive these divine oracles integrally, in the same sense in which they have been kept, and are still being kept, by this Roman Chair of Blessed Peter where, if man gathers not, he scatters. Remain firm and unshakably attached to this faith which, unless a man keep whole and entire, he shall undoubtedly be lost. *Ven. Pope Pius IX*

Every possible care must be taken to hold fast to that faith which has been believed *everywhere, always,* and by *everyone*. He is a genuine Catholic who continues steadfast in the faith, who resolves that he will believe those things - and *only* those things - which he is sure the Catholic Church has held universally and from ancient times. It is therefore an indispensable obligation for all Catholics to adhere to the faith of the Fathers, to preserve it, to die for it and, on the other hand, to detest the profane novelties of profane men, to dread them, to harass them, and to attack them. *St. Vincent of Lerins*

O keep that which is committed to thy trust, avoiding the profane novelties of words.
I St. Timothy 6:20

As long as you live and have breath in you, let no man change you! *Ecclesiasticus 33:21*

Continue in that doctrine which you have learned in Holy Church, neither adding nor subtracting from it.
Bl. Isaias

Whosoever does not continue in the doctrine of Christ does not have God. *II St. John 1:9*

MAN'S CONSCIENCE
WILL NOT SAVE HIM

For I have nothing on my conscience,
yet I am not thereby justified.

I Corinthians 4:4

That it is right for each individual to follow what is acceptable to his own religious creed makes the divine establishment of the Church of no consequence. Especially fatal to the salvation of souls is that erroneous opinion that liberty of conscience and liberty of worship is the proper right of every man. By our Apostolic authority, we condemn this evil opinion.

Ven. Pope Pius IX

It is quite unlawful to demand, to defend, or to grant unconditional freedom of thought, speech, writing, or worship, as though these were so many rights given man by nature. For if nature had really granted them, it would be lawful to refuse obedience to God, and there would be *no* restraint on human liberty, based on the principle that every man is free to profess any religion he may choose, or none at all. When a liberty such as we have described is offered, it is not liberty but the abject submission of the soul to sin. *Pope Leo XIII*

It is insanity to believe that liberty of conscience and liberty of worship are the inalienable rights of every citizen! From this foul-smelling fountain of Indifferentism flows the erroneous and absurd opinion - or rather *derangement* - that liberty of conscience must be asserted for everyone. This most pestilential error opens the door to complete liberty of opinions which work such widespread havoc both in Church and State. *Pope Gregory XVI*

By the fact that freedom of all forms of worship is proclaimed, truth is confused with error, and the holy and immaculate Spouse of Christ, outside which there can be no salvation, is placed on the same level with heretical sects and even with Jewish perfidy.
Pope Pius VII

That every man is free to embrace and profess whatever religion his reason approves of, is hereby condemned as error. *Ven. Pope Pius IX*

Thus saith the Lord God: "Woe to the foolish prophets who follow their own spirit!" *Ezechiel 13:3*

Man does not know whether he be worthy of love or hatred. *Ecclesiastes 9:1*

Work out your salvation with fear and trembling.
Philippians 2:12

For, it frequently happens that, when someone feels and believes himself to be very good, he is *not* good.
St. John Eudes

We must persuade ourselves that God cannot but hate sin. And if God hates sin, He must necessarily hate the sinner who makes league with sin.

St. Alphonsus Maria Liguori

To God the wicked and his wickedness are hateful *alike*.
Wisdom 14:9

In the Catholic Church there are both good and bad, but those who are separated from the Church *cannot* be good. For their very separation from the Church makes them bad according to Our Savior: "He who is not with Me is *against* Me." *St. Augustine*

Amongst Catholics, there are good and bad, but among heretics not *one* can be good.
St. Robert Bellarmine

A heretic is condemned by his own judgment: to unbelievers, nothing is clean; but their mind and their conscience are both defiled. *St. Titus 3:11; 1:15*

No heresy can ever be justifiable. *Pope Leo XIII*

Since this is true, then it seems to me that a serious error is being made by those who say that Jews and Moslems can be saved by keeping their own law, even if they do not believe in Jesus Christ, inasmuch as they imagine that their own belief is good, secure, and sufficient for their salvation and, in that belief, do many good deeds of justice. *No!* This is not enough!
Ven. Walter Hilton

If we were to say: "I give myself to the devil," we would not the less truly belong to the devil because we did not *feel* we belonged to him.

St. Louis Marie de Montfort

Some people suffer no remorse of conscience because they have not *got* a conscience.

St. Francis Xavier

The sin of this century is the loss of the sense of sin.

Pope John Paul II

He who opposes himself to the commands of God, even though he do so with a pious and friendly intention, such a one is nevertheless for this reason estranged from the Lord.   *St. Basil the Great*

Every way of a man seemeth right unto himself. The way of a fool is right in his own eyes. There is a way that seemeth right to a man, and the ends thereof lead to death.   *Proverbs 21:2; 12:15; 16:25*

There are ways which men call "right" that, in the end, plunge them into the depths of Hell.

St. Benedict

The road to Hell is paved with good intentions.

St. John Mary Vianney

All heretics who accept the authority of Holy Scripture are convinced they are cleaving to the truth, whereas they are pursuing their own errors. For all heretics try to justify the effrontery of their own vaporings.   *St. Augustine*

Heretics separate from the Church believing that they still hold the right doctrine. They lost their faith by some obstinate sin.   *St. Jerome*

However sinful I was, I always considered that I had some intention of serving God. Yet, for all that, I was shown the place in Hell the devil held in store for me!   *St. Teresa of Avila*

Although the sinner does not believe in Hell, he shall nevertheless go there, even though he neither believes in Hell nor even thinks about it.
                          St. Anthony Mary Claret

The devil always tries to deceive heretics by suggesting to them that they can be saved in their belief. Unhappy hope! I think the danger of eternal perdition, by dying separated from the Church, should be sufficient to convert *every* heretic.
                          St. Alphonsus Maria Liguori

Would that I might open to you the hearts of those who cut themselves off! Would that you might penetrate into their consciences! Then you would clearly see how many thorns are there! For, just as soil that is not touched becomes wild and ugly, so does the soul without spiritual cultivation bring forth weeds and thistles.   *St. John Chrysostom*

Those wretched heretics willfully blind themselves, and they claim that what they do is good, and they believe it to be so, yet without real confidence; for there is something within them that tells them they are wrong.   *St. Teresa of Avila*

Do not believe that our "professional unbelievers" are not without periods of clear perception in which they take account of the fact that they are deceiving themselves.   *St. Maximilian Mary Kolbe*

Behold: he who is unbelieving, his soul shall not be right in himself.   *Habacuc 2:4*

He is sinning, and he *knows* it!   *St. Titus 3:11*

That it is impossible you should know all your mortal sins is condemned as error.   *Pope Leo X*

For I know my iniquity, and my sin is always before me.   *Psalm 50:5*

Oh, what a torment it must be to the souls in Hell that they *knew* their error before they were lost, and that they are lost entirely through their own fault!
                    St. Alphonsus Maria Liguori

If a person wants to save his soul, he has to examine his conscience against the everlasting teaching of the Church.   *Pope John XXIII*

CATHOLICS JUDGE ALL OUTSIDE THE FAITH ETERNALLY LOST

***All may be judged who have
not believed the truth.***
II Thessalonians 2:11

It is not good to accept the person of the wicked, to decline from the truth of judgment. He who justifies the wicked is abominable before God.
Proverbs 18:5; 17:15

True Christian prudence makes us judge things as Jesus Christ judged them, and to speak and act as He did. ***St. Vincent de Paul***

Before you inquire, blame no man; and when you have inquired, reprove justly. ***Ecclesiasticus 11:7***

The love of neighbor has its limits. To outstep these limits by loving our neighbor as we love God would be an enormous crime. ***Catechism of Trent***

He who loves father or mother more than Me is not worthy of Me. And he who loves son or daughter more than Me is not worthy of Me.
St. Matthew 10:37

If, therefore, the whole Church come together into one place, and there come in someone who does not believe, he is convicted by everyone; he is judged by everyone. *I Corinthians 14:23-24*

Our Lord has clearly commanded us to regard as heathens those who will not hear the Church.
Ven. Pope Pius IX

He who does not believe is *already* judged.
St. John 3:18

It is hereby condemned as error that, although it is clearly established that a man is a heretic, you are not bound to denounce him, should you be unable to prove it. *Pope Alexander VII*

That we can have at least good hope for the salvation of all those who have never been in the true Church of Christ is hereby condemned as error.
Ven. Pope Pius IX

Judge those who forge schisms and who look to their own advantage rather than to the unity of the Church. Judge as well those who are outside the bounds of truth, namely: those who are outside the Church. *St. Irenaeus of Lyons*

Judge just judgment. Do you not judge that which is just even of yourselves? *St. Luke 12:57*

Do you not know that we shall judge angels? How much more the things of *this* world!
I Corinthians 6:3,2

We know that we are the children of God, and that all the rest of the world around us is under Satan's power and control. *I St. John 5:19*

By their fruits you will know them.
St. Matthew 7:16

"Judge not, and ye shall not be judged" (Lk. 6:37). What does this mean? Are we not to denounce those who sin? Why, then, does Paul say: "Reprove, entreat, rebuke!" (II Tim. 4:2), and "Reprove before everyone those who sin" (I Tim. 5:20)? Christ also said to Peter: "Rebuke him, and if he will not obey, tell the Church" (Mt. 18:15-17). Why, then, did He give His Apostles the power of the keys? For, if they are not to judge, they are without authority, and in vain have they received the power of binding and loosing. Besides, if this were the case, everything in the churches and cities and homes would come to an end. And, unless we correct our enemies, we shall never put an end to enmity, and everything would be turned up-side down. Therefore, let us take care to study the meaning of what is said here, so that no one may think that the remedies of our salvation are laws of disorder and confusion. For, Our Lord has made as clear as possible to those who have understanding the perfection of this law, saying: "First cast the beam out of thine own eye" (Lk. 6:42). You see, He does not forbid us to judge, but commands us first to remove the beam from our own eyes, and only then correct the faults of others.
St. John Chrysostom

CHAPTER SEVEN

ALL MEN HAVE SINNED
AND ARE WORTHY OF HELL

**For there is no just man upon earth
who does good and sins not.**
Ecclesiastes 7:21

There is no man who does not sin.   *III Kings 8:46*

We must realize that, to commit *no* sins, is really super-human, and pertains to God alone.
St. Gregory Nazianzen

It cannot be denied that, except for Jesus Christ and the Divine Mother who, by a singular privilege, have been free from all stain of sin, all other men - even the saints - have not been exempt from at least venial sins.   *St. Alphonsus Maria Liguori*

Who, except Mary, among the saints in Heaven, if asked whether he has committed sins, could say "No"? If it were within our power to bring together all the saints, and ask them whether they were without sin when they lived, would they not exclaim with one voice: "If we say that we have no sin, we deceive ourselves and the truth is not in us!" (I Jn.1:8)?
St. Augustine

For in many things we all offend.   *St. James 3:2*

No one is free from sin, not even the infant whose life on earth is merely one day.

Pope St. Leo the Great

Recall the anguished questions of Job: "Can mortal man be righteous before God? Can a man be pure before His maker? What is man, that he can be clean? Or he who is born of woman, that he can be righteous?" (Job 4:17; 14:15). And Proverbs: "Who can say: I have made my heart clean; I am pure from my sin?" (20:9). The Psalms ring out: "No man living is righteous before Thee! The wicked go astray from the womb; they err from their birth, speaking lies" (142:2; 57:3). All these texts pose the difficult problem of the universal situation of sin.

Pope John Paul II

Evil has spread from head to foot: from Pope to prelate; we have all deviated from the right way. Everything has been vitiated. *Pope Adrian VI*

From the least even to the greatest, from the prophet even to the priest, everyone deals deceitfully.

Jeremias 8:10

The fort is betrayed even by them that should have defended it. *St. John Fisher*

It should not frighten you that, in the Church, there are many bad and few good. For the Ark, a figure of the Church, was wide below and narrow above; and, at the summit, it measured only one cubit.

Pope St. Gregory the Great

Heaven is not clean in His sight. How much less are those who dwell in houses of clay?

Pope St. Clement I

We have all become unclean, and all our justices are like the rag of a menstruous woman.   *Isaias 64:6*

For there is no man who does not sin.

II Paralipomenon 6:36

Of ourselves, we are a Hell full of horrors, accursedness, sin, and abomination. We are all so many incarnate demons, Lucifers, and Antichrists, since everything in us is contrary to Christ. There is not a man in the world who, after having struggled for years with the infernal powers, would not be capable of losing his salvation in the last hour of his life.

St. John Eudes

Ah! How many Stars of the Firmament have we not seen fall miserably and, in the twinkling of an eye, lose all their height and brightness!

St. Louis Marie de Montfort

I have such a lot of sins. But who is without sins?

St. Bernadette Soubirous

I am *always* committing sin!   *Pope St. Gregory VII*

If anyone says a man, once justified, can avoid all sins, even venial sins, throughout his entire life without a special privilege of God, as the Church holds in regard to the Blessed Virgin, let him be anathema.

Council of Trent

CHAPTER EIGHT

MOST SOULS FORFEIT
THEIR SALVATION

For many are called, but few chosen.
St. Mark 20:16

Behold how many there are who are called, and how few who are chosen! And, if you have no care for yourself, your perdition is more certain than your amendment, especially since the way which leads to eternal life is so narrow.   *St. John of the Cross*

How narrow is the gate and how strait the way that leads to life, and few there are who find it.
St. Matthew 7:13-14

Do not be deceived; there are only two roads: one that leads to life and is narrow; the other that leads to death and is wide. There is no middle way.
St. Louis Marie de Montfort

Oh how much are worldlings deceived who think to go to Heaven by the wide way that leadeth only to perdition! The path to Heaven is narrow, nor can it be trodden without great toil; and therefore wrong is their way and assured their ruin who, after the testimony of so many saints, will not learn where to settle their footing.   *St. Robert Southwell*

The greater number of men still say to God: "Lord, we would rather be slaves of the devil and condemned to Hell than be Thy servants. Alas, the greatest number - we may say *nearly all* - offend and despise Thee, my Jesus. How many countries there are in which there are scarcely any Catholics, and all the rest either infidels or heretics! And all of them are certainly on the way to being lost.

St. Alphonsus Maria Liguori

What do you think? How many of the inhabitants of this city may perhaps be saved? Out of this thickly-populated city, not one hundred people will be saved! I doubt whether there will even be as many as that! *St. John Chrysostom*

Brethren, the just man shall scarcely be saved. What, then, will become of the sinner? *St. Arsenius*

If the just man shall scarcely be saved, where shall the ungodly sinner appear? *I St. Peter 4:18*

Scarcely *anyone* is saved.

St. Alphonsus Maria Liguori

If you would be quite sure of your salvation, strive to be among the fewest of the few. Do not follow the majority of mankind, but follow those who renounce the world and never relax their efforts day or night so that they may attain everlasting blessedness.

St. Anselm

So vast a number of miserable souls perish, and so comparatively few are saved! *St. Philip Neri*

The number of the saved is as few as the number of grapes left after the pickers have passed.

St. John Mary Vianney

It shall be as when a man gathers in the harvest, and the fruit that shall be left shall be as a single cluster of grapes; two or three berries on top of a bough; or four or five on the top of a tree. *Isaias 17:5-6*

The destiny of those dying on one day is that not as many as ten went straight to Heaven; and those cast into Hell were as numerous as snowflakes in winter.

Bl. Anna Maria Taigi

I tremble when I see how many souls are lost these days. They fall into Hell like leaves from the trees at the approach of winter. *St. John Mary Vianney*

Only a few will be saved; only few will go to Heaven. The greater part of mankind will be lost forever. *St. John Neumann*

There are a select few who are saved.

St. Thomas Aquinas

The number of the Elect is so small - *so small* - that, were we to know how small it is, we would faint away with grief. One here and there, scattered up and down the world! *St. Louis Marie de Montfort*

They shall be so few that they shall easily be counted, and a child shall write them down. *Isaias 10:19*

CHAPTER NINE

GOD'S MERCY CANNOT CONTRADICT HIS JUSTICE

He cannot deny Himself.
II St. Timothy 2:13

Mercy and wrath come quickly from the Lord, for mercy and wrath alike are with Him.
Ecclesiasticus 5:6; 16:12

What shall we say, then? Is there injustice with God? Far from it! For, He says to Moses: "I will have mercy on whom I will, and I will show mercy to whom I will" (Exod. 33:19). Therefore, God has mercy on whom He will, and whom He will He hardens. *Romans 9:14-20*

God shows His mercy for a certain time, and then He hardens the heart of the sinner by not having mercy on him. God is full of mercy, but He is not so stupid as to act without reason. To show mercy to those who continue to insult Him would be stupidity, not goodness. *St. Alphonsus Maria Liguori*

Misery upon misery to those who do not acknowledge that their misery comes from their own malice!
St. Francis de Sales

God, in the eternity of His changelessness, has prepared works of mercy and works of justice. For men who are to be justified, He has prepared merits; for those to be glorified, He has prepared rewards. But for the wicked, He has not prepared evil wills nor works, but just and eternal punishments. This is the eternal predestination taught us by Apostolic doctrine. *Pope Adrian I*

For the term "predestination" does not express some compulsory necessity of the human will, but foretells the eternal disposition, merciful and just, of a future divine operation. The Church, however, sings of mercy and judgment unto God, Whose predestination works in man in such a way that by a hidden, though not unjust, resolution of His will, He may either award mercy to the wretched, or weigh out due justice to the unrighteous. *St. Fulgentius*

The Lord searches all hearts, and understands all the thoughts of minds. If you seek Him, you shall find Him; but if you forsake Him, He will cast you off for ever. *I Paralipomenon 28:9*

The hand of God is upon all who seek Him in goodness, and His power and strength and wrath upon all who forsake Him. *Esdras 8:22*

Where shall miserable sinners fly when they see an angry Judge overhead, Hell open below, their sins on one side, and devils on the other dragging them to punishment? St. Peter said that, in the Judgment of Christ, the just man shall scarcely be saved. What shall become of the vindictive, the unchaste, of blasphemers and slanderers? What shall become of those whose entire *life* is opposed to Jesus Christ? Hence, we should not believe that God extends His mercy beyond the limits He has revealed in Scripture.

St. Alphonsus Maria Liguori

So that they may burn without end, the Lord by a very just judgment will give over to the punishment of eternal and inextinguishable fire the wicked who either did not know the way of the Lord or, knowing it, left it. *Pope Pelagius I*

Damnation is just. *Romans 3:8*

God saw the propriety of predestinating those who would obey and of reprobating those who would rise up against His majesty. The predestined were chosen by free grace, and the foreknown were reprobated with exact justice. If they could sin, so also could they abstain from sin. God violated the right of no one, since He forsook no one nor denied anyone that which is necessary. No one is excused for not knowing and loving Him. *Ven. Mary of Agreda*

It seems well at this point to reply briefly to the anxiety some feel when they see the great number of heathens and infidels in the universe. It should not be a cause of worry that so many are blinded by sins and vices and do not want to believe. Of all the people during the first epoch of the world's history, only Noah was found to be just. Nevertheless, he did not on that account cease to be holy and keep his faith. In the time of Abraham, there were still very few just men, but they did not lose their faith because they

141

lived among so many infidels. We know that Our Lord will not deny to anyone sufficient help for conversion; we also know that God has impressed upon all human intellects a knowledge of good and evil, and given man a free will whereby he can choose the one or the other. You will say: "But His punishment is eternal!" True, but that punishment is meted out by a God Who is not only just, but Justice itself. But what shall we say of those to whom the true faith has never been preached? They shall not suffer for infidelity, for this cannot be imputed to those who have never heard of the true faith. But they *can* be punished for sins they have committed against the Law which God has impressed on the hearts of all men, and for evil deeds committed out of malice.

Ven. Louis of Granada

Certainly, we do not hold that the wicked perish because they were unable to be good, but because they were *unwilling* to be good, and have remained in the mass of damnation either because of Original Sin or some actual sin.   *III Council of Valence*

To those who receive mercy, He gives it freely; from those who do not receive mercy, it is justly withheld.

St. Alphonsus Maria Liguori

To whomsoever grace is given, it is given mercifully; and from whom it is withheld, it is withheld justly, as a punishment of a previous sin or at least of Original Sin. Wherefore, they who are not liberated by grace, either because they are not yet able to hear the Word, or because they are unwilling to obey it, or because they did not receive that Bath of Regeneration which they might have received and been saved, are indeed justly condemned because they are not without sin: either that which they derived from their birth, or added from their own misconduct; "for all have sinned, and come short of the glory of God" (Romans 3:23). Surely, the lightest punishment of all will be given those who, besides the sin they brought with them originally, have added no other. Among the rest who *have* added sins, damnation will be so much the more tolerable as their wickedness was the less serious. ***St. Augustine***

So, the Savior goes on with His appointed task, although many perish. For, their destruction is not His aim, but is the consequence of their own ignorance. ***St. Thomas Aquinas***

The heathen who spurns the inspirations of God *in total ignorance of Revelation* sins by resisting God's grace. ***Pope Alexander VIII***

Despite the refusal of sinners to return to God, He does not cease to call them by so many interior inspirations, remorses of conscience, and terrors of chastisements. "My son," says the Lord, "I have almost lost My voice in calling you to repentance!" ***St. Alphonsus Maria Liguori***

I am weary of entreating thee. ***Jeremias 15:6***

My jaws have become hoarse. ***Psalm 68:4***

If your servant were to say: "Sir, for two years, I have been taking a candle to your son every morning so that he can get up and study, but he does nothing of the sort; he just leaves the candle burning on the night-stand and sleeps on," you would order him *not to take the candle any more*.

St. Benedict Joseph Labre

When God's mercies have reached their end He punishes, and pardons no more. God is merciful; but, as great as His mercy is, how many people He sends to Hell every day! God *is* merciful but He is also just; and He is therefore obliged to punish those who offend Him. When sins reach a certain number, God pardons no more. St. Basil, St. Cyril of Alexandria, St. Jerome, St. Ambrose, St. Augustine, St. John Chrysostom, and other Fathers teach that, according to the words of Scripture: "Thou hast ordered all things in measure and number and weight" (Wisdom 11:21), God has fixed for each person the number of sins He will pardon; and when this number is completed, He will pardon no more. God *does* bear with us, but not forever. When the time comes for vengeance, He punishes. How many God has sent to Hell for the first offense! St. Gregory relates that a child five years old was seized by the devil for having uttered a blasphemy and carried into Hell. Another of eight, after his first sin, died and was lost.

St. Alphonsus Maria Liguori

How many souls have been damned for a single mortal sin! *St. Ignatius of Loyola*

He Who has promised pardon to penitents has not promised tomorrow to sinners.

Pope St. Gregory the Great

Thus, those who are saved are saved because God willed them to be saved, and those who perish do so because they deserved to perish.

St. Prosper of Aquitaine

Nor will it do to say that "Faith is a Gift." At birth, man possesses the faculty of understanding, but he must bring it into action. *Pope St. Pius X*

Faith is a gift from God. And let no one have any doubt whatsoever that, while this gift is given to some, to others it is not given. Why it is not given to everyone ought not disturb the faithful; even if *no one* were delivered, there would be no just cause for finding fault with God! *St. Augustine*

It is suspect of heresy to say that faith and the reward of faith are a gift of the pure generosity of God. *Pope Clement XI*

Neither faith nor works shall free from eternal punishment any of those who die in mortal sin, even after any length of time whatever. It would seem that by the mercy of God all punishment of the damned comes to an end. Since, however, His mercy is ruled by His wisdom, it does not reach certain people who render themselves unworthy. And yet, the mercy of God is found even in them, in that they are punished less than they deserve. *St. Thomas Aquinas*

Some will say: "The fire, but not the punishment, is everlasting." Such is the language of the unbelieving! For what other purpose would God make this fire eternal except to chastise reprobates who are also immortal? These are not opinions controverted among theologians; they are dogmas of faith clearly revealed in the Sacred Scriptures. Moreover, the miserable wretches in Hell have no one to pity them. Not even God can compassionate them, for they are His enemies; neither can Mary, the Mother of Mercy; nor the angels or saints. On the contrary, they *rejoice* at their sufferings!   *St. Alphonsus Maria Liguori*

The Just shall rejoice when he shall see the revenge; he shall wash his hands in the blood of the sinner.
                                        Psalm 57:11

Although it might be Noah who sees his loved ones tormented in Hell, he dare not aid them. For there all compassion which arose from nature is extinguished. And, in order that those who earned Heaven might not be tormented by this pity, this very pity is extinguished, and they are enraged and on fire with wrath against their own blood kin.   *St. John Chrysostom*

Wherefore, all sinners are to be hated: even one's father or mother or kindred. For, it is our duty to hate in the sinner his being a sinner. Such hatred is perfect; the Prophet says: "I have hated them with a *perfect* hatred" (Ps. 138:22).   *St. Thomas Aquinas*

You have despised all My counsel, and have neglected My reprehensions. I also will *laugh* in your destruction, and I will *mock* you, when that shall come upon you which you feared!   *Proverbs 1:25-26*

146

The
BOOK OF
IGNORANT
NATIVES

CHAPTER ONE

NATIVES ON DESERT ISLANDS
ARE LOST TO DIVINE LIFE

*He who does not have the
Son does not have life.*
I St. John 5:12

Jesus saith: I am the way, and the truth, and the life:
no man cometh to the Father but by Me.
St. John 14:6

Not even the ones who are able to say that they did
not hear the Gospel of Christ will free themselves
from condemnation, since faith depends on hearing.
St. Augustine

No one may attain eternal life except through faith in
Our Lord Jesus Christ. **Pope Paul III**

Without Me, you can do *nothing*. **St. John 15:5**

No one comes to grace except him who knows the
Law. **St. Ambrose**

We must first *know* what is just before we can *do*
what is just. **St. Caesarius of Arles**

It is error to believe that, in the promise made to the
first man, there is enshrined the basis of *natural* jus-

tice whereby eternal life is promised for good works without any further qualification.   *Pope St. Pius V*

Acts which spring from natural goodness have only the appearance of virtue; they cannot last of themselves nor can they merit salvation. *Pope St. Pius X*

No matter how praiseworthy his actions might seem, he who is separated from the Catholic Church will never enjoy eternal life.   *Pope Gregory XVI*

Enemies of grace offer us examples of ungodly men who, although without the faith, abound in virtues where there is only the good of nature without the aid of grace. God *forbid* that there be true virtues in anyone unless he be just; and God forbid that he be truly just unless he live by the faith. All that is not of faith is *sin*. Where there is no knowledge of the eternal and unchangeable truth, virtue is false even in the best morality. The fact that a wicked man performs some good works does not mean that such works avail toward his eternal salvation.   *St. Augustine*

If anyone says that, without divine grace through Jesus Christ, a man can be justified by works done by his own natural powers: let him be anathema.
Council of Trent

The natural law is not enough. Man, all alone, is able to ruin himself, but not to save himself. Christ is necessary for us, and to live in His Spirit is our salvation. Keep this fundamental doctrine clearly in mind: Christ alone saves us.   *Pope Paul VI*

The idol made by hands is accursed, as well as him who made it. It was not enough for them to err about the knowledge of God but, whereas they lived in a great war of ignorance, they sacrifice their own children, so that they keep neither life nor marriage undefiled. For the worship of abominable idols is the cause, and the beginning, and the end of all evil.

Wisdom 14:8,22-27

The gods of the Gentiles are devils.   *Psalm 95:5*

Hell is the portion of all who die guilty of idolatry.

St. Wulfran

These unbelievers will be punished more tolerably because in some way they did naturally the things of the Law, having the work of the Law written in their hearts. *But even in this they were sinners* because, being men without the faith, they did not refer their works to that End to which they ought to have referred them.   *St. Augustine*

O God! Why art Thou not known? Why is this barbarous country not all converted to Thee? The savages once had some more-than-natural knowledge of the true God; but, being unwilling to revere God in their manners and actions, they lost the thought of Him, and they have become worse than beasts in His sight.   *St. John de Brebeuf*

But these men, like irrational beasts, tending to destruction by nature, blaspheming those things they do not know, shall perish in their corruption.

II St. Peter 2:12

CHAPTER TWO

GOD ENLIGHTENS
ALL MEN OF GOOD WILL

Everyone who is of the
truth hears My voice.
St. John 18:37

For, whosoever shall call upon the name of the Lord shall be saved. How, then, shall they call upon Him in Whom they have not believed? Or how shall they believe in Him of Whom they have not heard? Verily, their sound hath gone forth into all the earth, and their words unto the ends of the whole world.

Romans 10:11-18

Christ has come and enlightened *absolutely everyone* with His light. All parts of the world in every direction are illuminated by His teaching.

St. Athanasius

The Savior prophesied that His doctrine would be preached over the whole world, *wherever man has existed*, as a testimony to all nations. His Gospel has filled every country on which the sun shines; it has traversed every nation.   ***St. Eusebius of Caesaria***

The grace of God accompanies man from the womb to the tomb. We receive from God at every moment all that is necessary for us in the natural and supernatural order.   ***St. Maximilian Mary Kolbe***

Consequently, should someone put forward the case of a person who is brought up, for example, even among savages in the woods, it must most certainly be held that God would reveal to him what is necessary to be believed; even to direct some preacher of the faith to him, just as He sent Peter to Cornelius.

St. Thomas Aquinas

For I make doctrine to shine forth to everyone. Behold, I have labored for all who seek out the truth.

Ecclesiasticus 24:44-47

This is the true light, that enlightens *every man* who comes into this world.   *St. John 1:9*

This faith of ours has pervaded the entire earth by land and by sea, from the rising to the setting of the sun. This faith has illuminated with the light of divine knowledge *all* peoples, *all* races, *all* nations, howsoever barbarous they might be.

Ven. Pope Pius IX

The Catholic Church is settled in every place and in every country and in every city, established throughout the universe: in all nations, all cities, all villages, and in all places, filling the whole world!

St. Eusebius of Caesaria

No one can escape the eye of God. He sees the heart of every single person. He regards the minds of all men and the wishes conceived even in the hidden recesses of the heart.   *St. Cyprian*

Shall a man be hidden in secret places, and I not see him? saith the Lord. Do I not fill heaven and earth?
Jeremias 23:24

The means of salvation and sanctification are known by *all men*, and are necessary to everyone who wishes to be saved. The missionary mandate of salvation was made accessible to *everyone*.   *Pope Paul VI*

The Apostles went through the whole world, and courageously proclaimed everywhere the teaching of Christ.   *Pope Pius XII*

Even at the time of the Apostles, the Gospel was preached throughout the entire world.
St. Thomas Aquinas

The Gospel has come unto you as unto the whole world; the Gospel is preached in all creation under heaven.   *Colossians 1:5-6,23*

No one reaches the Heavenly Jerusalem except him who is on the road, although not everyone who is on the road will reach it. To be a Catholic Christian is to be on the road and walking in the way. For it was not God's will that the Church be hidden, so that no one might plead this excuse. It was foretold that the Church would be established throughout the entire earth. And it has been made visible to the whole world. Hence, it is true that the Church is hidden from nobody. It is not allowed for anyone *not* to know this Church; for which reason, according to the word of Jesus Christ, it is not possible that it be hidden.   *St. Augustine*

If any man will do the will of God, he shall know the doctrine. He who has My commandments and keeps them loves Me, and I will love him and will manifest Myself to him. *St. John 7:17; 14:21*

God our Savior will have all men to be saved, and to come to the knowledge of the truth.

I St. Timothy 2:4

Lest anyone say: "What about those who do not believe in Jesus Christ?" listen to what He adds: "I know Mine, *and Mine know Me*" (Jn. 10:14).

St. John Chrysostom

Everyone who wishes may find Thee, O Lord; but he who asks not, receives not. *St. Teresa of Avila*

God, therefore, has imposed on us a law which our strength is unable to observe, so that we may have recourse to Him and, by prayer, obtain the strength to fulfill it. Prayer, the asking for graces, is necessary as a means without which salvation is absolutely impossible on the part of everyone who has attained the use of reason. He who prays is certainly saved; he who does not pray is certainly lost!

St. Alphonsus Maria Liguori

CHAPTER THREE

IGNORANCE HAS ONLY ITSELF TO BLAME FOR ALL ETERNITY

He who is of God hears the words of God. Therefore, you hear them not, because you are not of God.
St. John 8:47

That whatever is done through ignorance must not be considered a sin, is hereby condemned as error.
Pope Innocent II

It does not suffice to say: "If I had known that such a thing were forbidden by the law of God, I would have conformed." St. Paul, in persecuting Christians, previous to his conversion, did not think that he was committing evil; the same may be said of Jews who persecuted and crucified Christ. And yet, Saint Paul and these Jews were *not* innocent and excusable. If they had died in that state, they would never have been saved. Hence, St. Paul, despite the good faith he acted on, acknowledges that he was at that time a blasphemer, and unjust: a persecutor of the Church. If, therefore, a person be ignorant of what is commanded or forbidden because he has not studied the law of God, his ignorance does not excuse him from sin. ***St. Alphonsus Maria Liguori***

155

If ignorance is not a sin, then Saul did not sin when he persecuted the Church, because he surely did this in ignorance. Therefore, he should not have said: "I obtained the *mercy* of God" (I Tim. 1:13), but rather "I received my *reward*." **St. Bernard**

It may be true that there are, in the remotest parts of the world, some people who have not yet seen the light of the Savior. Certainly, God's manifold and ineffable goodness has always provided, and still provides, for all mankind in such a way that *not one* of the reprobates can find an excuse as though he had been refused the light of truth.
St. Prosper of Aquitaine

But if Christ "enlightens every man who comes into this world" (Jn. 1:9) why have so many remained unenlightened? How then does Christ "enlighten every man"? He does so, as far as in Him lies. For grace is poured out over everyone. It is easily attainable by all. However, if some people, willfully shutting the eyes of their mind, do not wish to receive the light, then their darkness arises from their own wickedness in cutting themselves off from grace. Whoever does not wish to enjoy these gifts may blame himself for his blindness. **St. John Chrysostom**

The Gentiles walk in vanity, having their understanding darkened, being alienated from the life of God through the ignorance in them because of the blindness of their hearts. **Ephesians 4:17-18**

For their own malice blinded them. **Wisdom 2:21**

Those who keep their eyes shut cannot see. God made you without your knowledge, but He does not justify you without your willing it. Refusal to hear the truth leads to sin, and that sin itself is punishment for the preceding sin. Every sinner is inexcusable *whether he knows it or not*. For ignorance itself, in those who do not want to know, is without doubt a sin; and, in those unable to know, is the penalty of sin. In neither case, then, is there a just excuse, but in both cases there is a just condemnation.

St. Augustine

It follows that ignorance has the nature of mortal sin on account of either a preceding negligence, or the consequent result; and, for this reason, ignorance is reckoned one of the general causes of sin. *All* sin proceeds from ignorance.   *St. Thomas Aquinas*

I will destroy men off the face of the earth, saith the Lord: those who turn away from following after the Lord, *and* those who have not sought after the Lord nor searched after Him.   *Sophonias 1:3,6*

Those who perish do not receive the love of truth in order that they might be saved. Therefore, God will send them the operation of error, to believe lying, so that all may be judged who have not believed the truth but have consented to iniquity.

II Thessalonians 2:10-11

No one is lost without knowing it, and no one is deceived without wanting to be.   *St. Teresa of Avila*

But why is it that so many men are ignorant, even at this day? This is the reason: "The light has come into the world, but men loved darkness rather than the light" (Jn. 3:19). They have not known Him, and do not know Him, because they do not *want* to know Him, loving instead the darkness of sin rather than the light of grace.   *St. Alphonsus Maria Liguori*

Unbelief has the character of guilt from resisting the faith, rather than from mere absence of the faith.
                                    St. Thomas Aquinas

If the Son of God will have all men to be saved, how is it that so many suffer the torments of Hell? I answer in one word: *They wish it.* He sends preachers of His Gospel to all parts of the world to proclaim: "He who believes, and is baptized, shall be saved." And if any are unwilling to enter on this way, they perish by their own fault and not by the lack of will on the part of the Redeemer. For an hour the perfidious Jews exulted over Christ in His sufferings; Judas for an hour enjoyed the price of his avarice; for an hour Pilate gloried that he had regained the friendship of Herod and not lost the friendship of Caesar. But for nearly two thousand years they have *all* been suffering the torments of Hell, and their cries of despair will be heard for ever and ever.
                                    St. Robert Bellarmine

Innumerable souls are miserably lost through ignorance of religion, the source of every other calamity.
                                    St. Frances Xavier Cabrini

If you are ignorant of the truths of the faith, you are obliged to learn them. Every Christian is bound to learn the Creed, the Our Father, or the Hail Mary under pain of mortal sin. Many have no idea of the Most Holy Trinity, the Incarnation, mortal sin, Judgment, Paradise, Hell, or Eternity; and this deplorable ignorance damns them.

St. Alphonsus Maria Liguori

Reflect on the ruin of souls wrought by this single cause: ignorance of truths which must be known by all men alike in order that they may attain eternal salvation. This we solemnly affirm: the majority of those condemned to eternal punishment fall into everlasting misfortune through ignorance of the Mysteries of the faith, which must necessarily be known and believed by all who belong to the Elect.

Pope St. Pius X

Both educated and simple folk are bound to *explicit* faith in the mysteries of Christ, chiefly those publicly proclaimed and observed throughout the universal Church. *St. Thomas Aquinas*

This is eternal life: that they may *know* Thee, the only true God, and Jesus Christ, Whom Thou hast sent. *St. John 17:3*

My Jesus, he who does not love Thee proves that he does not know Thee. *St. Teresa of Avila*

Poor creature! You do not know God; neither can you love Him! *St. Alphonsus Maria Liguori*

Is it possible for a man to love what he does not know? *St. Louis Marie de Montfort*

But if any man know not, he shall not *be* known. *I Corinthians 14:38*

To be unknown by the Lord is to perish. *St. Augustine*

I never knew you; depart from Me, you who work iniquity! *St. Matthew 7:23*

My heart is penetrated with grief when I think of the almost infinite number of souls who are damned for lack of knowing the true God and the Christian religion. The greatest misfortune, O my God, is not to know Thee, and the greatest punishment not to love Thee. *St. Louis Marie de Montfort*

Before their Baptism, certain Japanese were greatly troubled by a hateful scruple: that God did not appear merciful, because He had never made Himself known to the Japanese people before, especially that those who had not worshipped God were doomed to everlasting Hell. They grieve over the fate of their departed children, parents, and relatives; so they ask if there is any way to free them by prayer from the eternal misery. And I am obliged to answer: *there is absolutely none.* *St. Francis Xavier*

The excuse of ignorance is denied those who know the commandments of God, but neither will those who do *not* know be without punishment. "For, as many as have sinned outside the law shall also perish outside the law" (Romans 2:12). Without faith in Christ, no man can be delivered; therefore, they will be judged in such a way that they perish. "The servant who does not know his Lord's will, and who commits things worthy of stripes, shall be beaten with few stripes; whereas, the servant who knows his Lord's will, shall be beaten with many stripes" (Lk. 12:47-48). Observe here that it is a more serious matter for a man to sin with knowledge than in ignorance. And yet, we must not take refuge on this account to shades of ignorance, to find our excuse therein. Even ignorance which belongs to them who are, as-it-were, *simply* ignorant does not excuse anyone so as to exempt him from eternal fire, even were his failure to believe the result of *not having heard at all* what he should believe. It was not said without reason: "Pour out Thy wrath upon the nations who have not known Thee" (Psalm 78:6), and "He shall come from Heaven in a flame of fire to take vengeance on those who do not know God" (Thess. II 1:7-8).   *St. Augustine*

Christ says that not only those who do evil, but likewise those who omit to do the good commanded to be done, shall suffer eternal punishment. You who know, or ought to know, are inexcusable!

St. Francis de Sales

Do not think that justice consists merely in not doing evil, for not to do good is also evil, and the law may be transgressed in both ways.　　*St. Athanasius*

Before a man comes to the age of reason, the lack of years excuses him from mortal sin. But when he begins the use of reason, he is not entirely excused from the guilt of venial or mortal sin. Now, the first thing which occurs to a man at that age is to deliberate concerning himself. And if he then directs himself to the Due end, he will by grace receive the remission of Original Sin; whereas, if he does not, at that time, direct himself to the Due End as far as he is capable of discretion at that age, he sins *mortally*, by not doing that which is within his power.

St. Thomas Aquinas

The crime of ignoring the Lord is not less than that of offending Him. Ignorance of God is sufficient reason for punishment !　　*Minucius Felix*

And since they did not like God in their knowledge, He delivered them up to a reprobate sense, being, as they were, filled with all iniquity.　*Romans 1:28-29*

And if our Gospel be hidden, it is hidden from those who are perishing, in whom the god of this world has blinded the minds of unbelievers, in order that the light of the Gospel should not shine unto them.

II Corinthians 4:3-4

Because of these things, the anger of God comes upon the children of unbelief.　　*Ephesians 5:6*

An ignorant person is like a dying man lying uncon-
scious: he does not know either the malice of sin or
the value of his soul. He goes from sin to sin, like a
rag dragged through the mire.

St. John Mary Vianney

Perhaps he who asserts that a person cannot sin
through ignorance never prays for his ignorances,
but laughs at the prophet who prays: "O Lord, remember not the sins of my ignorances!" (Ps. 24:7).
Perhaps he even reproves God, Who requires sat-
isfaction for the sin of ignorance, for in Leviticus He
speaks of "sin through ignorance." If ignorance were
never a sin, why is it that the High Priest entered the
second tabernacle with blood, which he offered "for
his own ignorance and for the ignorance of the people" (Heb. 9:7)? If one never sins through ignorance,
then what do we hold against those who killed the
Apostles, since they truly did not know that to kill
them was evil but rather thought that they were "doing a service to God" (Jn. 16:2). Thus, also, Our Savior prayed in vain on the cross for those who crucified Him since, as He Himself testifies, they were ignorant of what they were doing (Lk. 23:34) and thus
they did not sin at all! Neither should anyone suspect
that the Apostle could have lied when he said: "For,
if they had known it, they would never have crucified the Lord" (I Corinth. 2:8). Is it not sufficiently
clear, from these passages, in what great ignorance
the man lies who does not know that one can sometimes sin through ignorance?   *St. Bernard*

Hasten to know, therefore, in what way forgiveness
of sins and hope of inheriting the good things which

have been promised shall be yours. For there is no way but this: to become acquainted with Christ, to be washed in the fountain prophesied for the remission of sins, and, for the rest, to live sinless lives.

St. Justin the Martyr

O Mary, merciful Refuge of Sinners! Behold how many souls are lost every hour! Behold the countless millions of those who live in barbarous regions, and do not know Jesus Christ. See, too, how many others are far from the bosom of Mother Church: Catholic, Apostolic, Roman! O Mary, let not the Precious Blood and fruits of Redemption be lost for so many souls. Grant that heavenly light may enlighten and enkindle so many cold hearts. Obtain the grace for all pagans, Jews, heretics, and schismatics to receive supernatural light and enter into the bosom of the true Church. Hear the prayer of the Supreme Pontiff that all nations may be united in the one faith, that they may know and love Jesus Christ the blessed fruit of thy womb. Then all men shall love thee also, who art the salvation of the world, dispenser of the treasures of God. And, glorifying thee who, by means of thy Rosary, dost trample upon all heresies, they shall acknowledge that it is thou who givest life to all nations: a fulfillment of the prophecy: "All generations shall call me blessed." *Amen.*

Pope Pius XI

REFERENCES

The sources of Scriptural selections are obviated by inclusion in the text, and will not be repeated herein. Generally, the Douay-Rheims has been favored; however, other Catholic editions have also been excerpted.

PAGE - AUTHOR - REFERENCE

13

John Mary: VHM, *cf.* p.162

Bernardine: "On the Birth of the Blessed Virgin," ch.8, vol. IV, p.96, Lyons: 1650; Fr. M.J. Scheeben, MARIOLOGY, vol. II, St. Louis: B. Herder, 1948, p.271; VOS 143; SERMONS, St. Alphonsus Maria Liguori, Dublin: Grace & Co. 1845, p.132; "On the Nativity of the Blessed Virgin," BVM, vol. II, p.236

Leo XIII: "Jucunda Semper," Sept. 8th, 1894, ACTA APOSTOLICAE SEDIS, Vatican Press, Rome; "Adjutricem Populi," PTL:113, 171

14

Bernard: "The Aqueduct," PL 183:437; VOS p.143-144

John: LSW p.90

Irenaeus: "Against Heresies," Bk. III:22, v.19; PG 7:959, and 1175; Scheeben, MARIOLOGY, II, p.204; JUR:vol. I: 224

William Joseph: MCL p. 7, 15

15

Louis Marie: TDM p.25-26

Peter Julian: VOS p.137; OUR LADY OF THE MOST BLESSED SACRAMENT, NY: Eymard League, 1930, p.10

Thomas: "Studies of the Hail Mary," Parmensi: 1852, vol. XVI, p.133

Pius IX: "Ubi Primum," PTL:23
Bernard: "On the Twelve Privileges of the Blessed Virgin Mary," no.2, PL 183:429
William Joseph: MCL pp. 109, 25
Leo XIII: Op. cit.

16

Louis Marie: SLM p.159
Pius X: "Ad Diem Illum Laetissim.," PTL:235; Allocution of Nov.12, 1910, PTL:256
Peter Julian: OUR LADY OF THE MOST BLESSED SACRAMENT, NY: Eymard League, 1930, p.1-3
Bernard: "On the Feast of Pentecost," Sermon II, ch.4, PL 183; "On the Assumption," PL 183:429; GM 243

17

Alphonsus Maria: MCH p.363
Idelphonsus: IPM p.62; PL 53:110
John Paul II: LOR, *cf.* April 25, '83, p.9-10

18

Augustine: "De Sanctis," Serm. 18; TGC, vol. IV, p.24
Leo XIII: "Adjutricem Populi," BVM, Vol.II, p.182
Pius X: Op. cit., PTL:230
Ambrose: GM p.48, VOS p.135
Bernard: IPM p.25; PL 183

19

Hilary: GM p.223; VOS p.139
Antoninus: "On the Blessed Virgin," GM p.243; IPM p.28
Bonaventure: IPM p.16
Ignatius: VHM p.123
Louis Marie: SOR p.78
John: GM p.225; DDP p.414
Andrew: "Dormition of the Holy God-Bearer," Sermon III, PG 97:700; GM p.277

20

Alphonsus Maria: GM p.240
Bernard: AHM p.127; PL 183
John: LSW p.334-335
Louis Marie: TDM p.225

21

William Joseph: OUR KNOWLEDGE OF MARY, Kirkwood, MO: Maryhurst Press, 1930, p.4
Bonaventure: "Psalter of the Blessed Virgin Mary," Ps.116; DDP p.413; IPM p.90; GM p.221, 170; *cf.* also SOR p.30
Pius XII: PTC:969

22

Maximilian Mary: *Cf.* International Center, Militia of the Immaculate, Rome
Louis Marie: TDM pp.19-20, 30, 139 ff
Maximilian Mary: ICS p.85
John: *cf.* AHM p.78

24

Pius IX: "Singulari Quidem," PTC:222
IV Lateran: DNZ:430
Cyprian: UOC; CSL:214
Origen: "On Josue," homily III:5; GCW; FOC p.134
Pius IX: OUR GLORIOUS POPES, Slaves of the Immaculate Heart of Mary, Cambridge, MA: 1955, p.168

25

Pius XI: "Mortalium Animos," PTC:873
Louis Marie: HMG p.107
Pius X: "Supremi Apostolatus," PTC:654; "Jucunda Sane," PTC:668
Edmund: LFS p.177
Fulgentius: "To Euthymius, On the Remission of Sins," Bk. I, ch.19, no.2, PL 65:527; *cf.* also JUR vol.III:2251a
Boniface VIII: "Unam Sanctam," DNZ:468

26

Pius IX: "Singulari Quadem," DNZ:1647

John Paul II: *The Wanderer*, May 14, 1992, p.10, col.4

John Paul I: First Address To College Of Cardinals, August 27, 1978; CATHOLIC ALMANAC, ed. Fr. Felician Foy, OFM, 1979, p.54

Sylvester II: Profession of Faith made as Archbp. of Rheims, June, 991; *cf.* LETTERS OF GERBERT, NY: Columbia University Press, 1961, p.224

Benedict XV: RAC:484

27

Paul VI: General Audiences: May 15 and June 12, 1974; *The Wanderer*, May 30 and July 4, 1975; LOR June 8, 1972; TCH pp.12, 14, 18, 83, 123, 165; quoting St. Thomas Aquinas, ST III, 73, 3 and St. Augustine, 27:6, PL 33:85, PL 35:1618

Pius XII: PTC:1351

28

Pius IX: "Ubi Primum," December 17, 1847

Pius XI: "Dobbiamo Intrattenerla," PTC:907

John Paul II: LOR, Oct. 12, 1981, p.6

Catechism: COT p.105-106

Augustine: Epistle 141:5, CSL 41:238

29

Gregory XVI: "Perlatum Ad Nos," PTC:186

Edmund: LFS p.175-176

Augustine: "Treatise on John," PL 35:1618; *idem* no.26, PL 35:1568; Sermon XCI, PL 38:567

John Paul II: "Redemptoris Hominis," VII

Pius XII "Humani Generis," PTC:1282

30

John XXIII: "Quotiescumque Nobis," June 29, 1961

William Joseph: MCL p.47

Leo XIII: "Annum Ingressi Sumus," PTC:652-653; "Tamet-si," PTC:647

31
Eugene IV: "Cantata Domino," DNZ:714

32
Gregory XVI: "Perlatum Ad Nos," PTC:186; "Summo Jugi-ter," PTC:158
Clement VI: "Super Quisbudam," DNZ:570 b,1
Pius XII: "Meninisse Juvat," PTC:1547 *ff.*
Alphonsus Maria: CAS p.57
Pius IX: PTC:254
Augustine: "To the People of Caesaria," Sermon VI, CSL I-II, p.526 *ff.*, Vienna: C. Gerold's Son; PL 43:695; JUR *cf.* vol. III: 1535 & 1858; GOH p.10

33
Florence: "Decree for the Jacobites," DNZ:714
Peter Canisius: CATECHISM, "Creed": Art.9; GOH p.13-14
John Mary: SPIRIT OF THE CURE D'ARS, Bowden, 1864
Robert: LFB pp.19-20, 259

34
Catherine: SCS pp.200, 201, 380
Fulgentius: "On the Faith, to Peter," ch.38, PL 65:704
Catechism: COT p.515-517
Pius XII: RAC:626

36
Gregory XVI: "Caritate Christi," PTC:147
I Vatican: "On Faith," ch.3, DNZ:1792 and 1793
Trent: "On Justification," ch.7, DNZ:799
Alphonsus Maria: *cf.* TRE
Pius IX: "Qui Pluribus," PTC.193

37

Eugene IV: "Exultate Deo," DNZ:695
Adrian II: "Actio I," DNZ:171, n.1
Pius IX: "Nostis et Nobiscum," December 8, 1849
Pius VIII: *Cf.* RECOLLECTIONS OF THE LAST FOUR POPES, Cardinal Nicholas Wiseman, London: 1858
Pius XII: "Ad Apostolorum Principis," PTC:1536
Gregory XIII: "Profession of Faith," DNZ:1085; DNZ:1000
Elizabeth Ann: MOTHER SETON: Saint Elizabeth of New York, Fr. Leonard Feeney, Cambridge: Ravengate Press, 1975

38

Andrew: SKL p.129
Robert: "Christian Doctrine," Introduction
Alphonsus Maria: PGW p.376
Augustine: *cf.* "On Christian Doctrine," ch.4, PL 34; RSS
Athanasian Creed: DNZ:39-40

39

Patrick: THE WRITINGS OF ST. PATRICK, White, 1954
Francis: SAINTS AND BLESSEDS OF THE THIRD ORDER OF ST. FRANCIS, Fr. Louis Biersack, OFM Cap., Paterson, NJ: St. Anthony Guild Press, 1943, p.35
Trent: Tridentine Profession of Faith, DNZ:1000
Pius IV: from the Bull "Injunctum Nobis," DNZ:1000
I Vatican: *idem*, note 1

40

Gregory the Great: *Cf.* "Moralia," ch.14:5; PL 75
Nilus: Epistle 28, Allatius, Rome: 1668, L.III, p.304; PG 79, FOC p.182
Fulgentius: Epistle 17:51; JUR vol.III:2244
Alphonsus Maria: TRE p.86-87

41

John Chrysostom: "On the Consolation of Death," Sermon 2, PG 56:299
John Bosco: DON BOSCO: Spiritual Portrait, Phelan: 1963

Peter: THE ROMAN MARTYROLOGY, ed. J. B. O'Connell, 4th typical edition, approved by Pope Benedict XV, Westminster, MD: Newman Press, 1962, p.37
George: VOM p.239
Gregory the Great: "Moralia," 34:19, PL 75:509; SKL p.61
Pius X: *Cf.* GOH p.17
Prosper: "The Call of All Nations," Bk. I:7, JUR vol.III:2042
Trent: "On Justification," ch.15; *cf.* DNZ:808, 837
Benedict Joseph. *Cf.* BJL

42

Alphonsus Maria: IBI p.407 *ff.*
Francis: SKL p.142

43

I Lateran: HOC
Martin I: Canon 18, Lateran Council, DNZ: 271-272
Cyprian: Epistle 69:4, CSL:3753

44

Augustine: "Contra Epistolam Parmeniani," Bk. II, ch.2, no. 25; PL 44; *idem*, no.25, FOC p.177, PL 43:33; CSL vol.LI (1908); "Contra Litter. Petil. Donat.," Bk. II, FOC *cf.* p.311
Trent: "Decree on Edition and Use of the Sacred Books," Session IV, DNZ:786
Thomas: STL II-II, Q.10, art.3, *ff*; art.6
John: LSW p.55

45

Alphonsus Maria: *cf.* TRE ch.16
Pius IX: *From The Housetops*, Still River, MA: 1977, vol. V, p.17, no.1
VII Carthage: PL 4:1051; CSL vol.III, Pt.1 (1868); SCN vol. I, p.951; JUR vol.I:600
Innocent IV: "Ad Extirpanda," *cf.* ISABELLA OF SPAIN, Dr. Wm. Thos. Walsh, London: Sheed & Ward, 1935, p.239
Pius IX: PTC
Leo the Great: Sermon 75, PL 54:400; SS vol.III p.44, no.4

Innocent IV: THE REGISTERS OF INNOCENT IV, Berger, Paris: 1881
St. Augustine: "On Heresies," no.88; PL 42

46

Edmund: LFS p.176
Catechism: COT pp. 361, 369
Gregory the Great: "Homilies on the Gospels," II:30, JUR vol.III:2333
Augustine: *Cf.* SS
Catherine: RCH vol.I, p.477-479

47

Frances Xavier Cabrini: TRAVELS, pp.84, 71
Peter Julian: THE REAL PRESENCE, NY: Blessed Sacrament Fathers, 1938, p.245
Alphonsus Maria: MCH p.387; CAS p.66, no.19
Augustine: "On Baptism, Against the Donatists," Bk. IV, ch.25, no.32, CSL vol.LI (1908)

48

IV Lateran: *Cf.* RCH
Teresa: SKL p.117
Therese: SKL p.27-28, LFB p.10
Louis: *Cf.* THE LIFE OF ST. LOUIS, John of Joinville, NY: Sheed & Ward, 1955
John: "Ad Popul. Ant." homily I, PGW p.409-410

49

Augustine: Sermon XCI, PL 38:567

50

Barnabas: TAF; attributed to St. Barnabas
Leo the Great: Sermon CLXVIII; BVM vol.II, p.119
Vincent: A CHRISTOLOGY: From the Sermons of St. Vincent Ferrer, London: Blackfriars Publications, 1954 p.82

51

Gregory IX: "Epistle to the Hierarchy of Germany," in 1233 A.D., ANNALES ECCLESIASTICI, Cardinal Caesar Baronius, ed. August Theiner, 1864, vol.I

Innocent III: "Epistle to the Hierarchy of France," July 15, 1205, PL 215

Thomas: "De Regimine Judaeorum"

Leo VII: REG. PONTIF., vol.I:3597, Jaffe, Leipzig: 1888

Augustine: "Against the Jews," PL 42:51

Innocent III: "Epistle to the Count of Nevers," 1208, PL 215

52

Vincent: STUDY OF THE SERMONS OF ST. VINCENT FERRER, Chabas, Madrid: 1902

Justin: FLORILEGIUM PATRISTICUM, Rauschen, 1911

Agobard: AOJ

53

Florence: "Decree for the Jacobites," DNZ:712

Ambrose: PAD p.316; TGC vol.III, p.311, on Matthew 27:51

54

Bernard: SS

Bernardine: AOJ

Elvira: Canon 50, JUR vol.I:611z; SCN vol.II

John: "Six Homilies Against the Jews," AOJ

Augustine: AOJ; *cf.* also JUR vol.III:1536

55

Gregory: AOJ

Basil:"On Prayer," Sermon IX, PG 32; SS vol.II p.384

Alphonsus Maria: PAD P.444

57

Paul VI. *Cf.* TCH p.82

II Vatican: "Decree on Ecumenism," ch.1; a literal rendering from the Latin original

Pius XI: "Mortalium Animos," PTC:872

Leo XIII: "Annum Ingressi Sumus," PTC:652

58

Cyprian: "Epistle to Magnus," 69:3, JUR vol.I:589
Hilary: "On Psalm 121," no.5; CSL vol. XXII, Vienna: 1891;
PL 9; FOC p.154
Paul VI: *cf.* TCH; "Ecclesiam Suam," Boston: St. Paul Ed.
Pius XII: "Mystici Corporis," PTC:1022 *ff.*

59

Paul VI: General Audience, June 12, 1974; LOR; *The Wanderer*, July 4, 1974, p.1; *cf.* also TCH p.123
John Paul II: Address to the Third General Assembly of Latin American Bishops, Jan. 28, 1979; *National Catholic Register*, L.A.,CA: Feb. 11, 1979
John Paul I: General Audience, Sept. 13, 1978, LOR no.38;
THE MESSAGE OF JOHN PAUL I, Boston: St. Paul Editions, 1978, p.106-107
Athanasius: "Discourse Against the Arians," Bk. I, ch.1, no.
1, PG 26:11
Augustine: Enchiridion, no.1, *cf.* THE NATURE OF THE
MYSTICAL BODY, Fr. Ernest Mura, CM, St. Louis: B. Herder, 1963, p.280
John Mary: THE CURE D'ARS, Msgr. Francis Trochu, London: Burns & Oates, 1955, p.145

60

Pacian: "Epistle to Sympronium," Bk. I:4, JUR vol.II:1243
Ignatius: PG 5:643
Athanasius: "Epistle to Serapion," Bk. I:28, PG 26:522
John: *cf.* LJS p.5
Cyprian: "Epistle to Antonianus," 52; FOC p.33
Robert: "On the Church Militant"
Paul VI: *Cf.* TCH

61

Tertullian: "On Baptism," ch.15, PL 1:1216; JUR vol.I:308
Augustine: "Against Faustus the Manichean," no.4; *cf.* PL
42: 207; CSL vol.:1 (1891); FOC *cf.* p.351

Leo XIII: "Satis Cognitum," PTC:616
Jerome: *Cf.* "Commentary on Matthew," PL 26
Catechism: COT p.107
Cyprian: UOC ch.9-13; ANL

62

Francis: *From The Housetops*, Still River, MA: 1977, vol.V, no.2, inside back cover
Trent: "On Justification," Canon 20; DNZ:830
Pius IX: *Cf.* RAC:626; "Syllabus of Errors," V:21, DNZ: 1721; III:16, DNZ:1716; III:18, DNZ:1718
I Vatican: "On Faith," Canon 6, DNZ:1815
Gregory XVI: "Mirari Vos," PTC:164

63

Leo XIII: "Satis Cognitum," PTC:1566
Boniface I: "Ep. ad Thessalon.," LAF vol.IX:57; FOC p. 324
John Paul II: "Address to the Theologians of Spain," LOR, December 20, 1982, p.4, col.1, no.5; "To the Religious of Sao Paolo," July 3, 1980, LOR, June 21, 1980 and November 9, 1981, p.9, col.1

64

Paul VI: "Evangelii Nuntiandi," no.16, December 8, 1975
Ambrose: "On Luke," Book VI:101, JUR vol.II: 1304
Epiphanius: "Against All Heresies," no.80, FOC p.171
Jerome: FOC p.75, note 4
Tertullian: "Objection Against Heretics," no.14, PL 2:12; CSL Vienna: 1942, p.1; FOC p.365

65

Optatus: "Schism of the Donatists," Bk.I, no's.6, 10; LAF vol. II; PL 11; CSL vol.XXVI, Vienna: 1893; FOC p.158
Ambrose: "Expl. of Luke" ch.7, 91-95; PL 15; SS vol. II, p.85
Hilary: "On Psalm 121," no.5; CSL vol.XXII, Vienna: 1891; PL 9; FOC p.154
Leo the Great: *Cf.* "Sermon on the Passion," PL 54
Augustine: "On the Trinity," no.6, CORPUS CHRISTIANO-RUM, Fr. Glorie, vol.50 (1968); FOC p.383

66

John Paul II: "To the National Meeting of Italian Catholic Action," LOR, July 21, 1980

Pius X: "Address on the Beatification of Joan of Arc," April, 1909, OUR GLORIOUS POPES, Cambridge, MA: Slaves of the Immaculate Heart of Mary, 1955, p.179

Lactantius: "Divine Institutions," Bk.IV, ch.30, no.11-12, PL 6:542; PTC:873

67

Alphonsus Maria: *Cf.* TRE

John XXIII: "Ad Petri Cathedram," *cf.* ACTA APOSTOLICAE SEDIS, Rome: no.50

Bridget: BOOK OF REVELATIONS, St. Bridget of Sweden, ed. Cardinal John Torquemada, Rome: 1488

Pius IX: "Singulari Quidem," PTC:222

Alphonsus Maria: *Cf.* TRE

Augustine: "Faith and the Creed," PL 40:181

Leo III: "Providentissimus Deus," Section V, RSS

68

Pius IX: "Mit Brennender Sorge," PTC:934, 940; "Lux Veritatis," PTC:923

II Vatican: "Dei Verbum," ch.2:10; VATICAN COUNCIL II, ed. Fr. Austin Flannery, OP, Northport, NY: Costello Publishing Co., 1975, p.755

John Paul II: "Homily for World Mission Sunday," LOR, November 26, 1979

Gregory XVI: "Mirari Vos," PTC:164

Hilary: "Commentary on Matthew," Bk.XII:1, t.1

Irenaeus: "Against Heresies," Bk.V, ch.20, PG 7; SAINT IRENAEUS AGAINST HERESIES, Cambridge: 1857, vol.II; FOC p.193

69

Ambrose: "On Psalm 118: Lamed," XIX; FOC p.70-71

Alphonsus Maria: TRE p.440-461

Cyprian: "On Re-Baptism," Treatise X; JUR vol.I:601; (contained in the works of St. Cyprian; questionable authorship)
Cyril: *cf.* "On the True Faith," PG 76:1204
Epiphanius: "Anaceph.," Bk.II, FOC *cf.* p.66-67
Cyprian: UOC ch.XXIII; *cf.* also "Ad Plebem, de Quinque Presbyteris," Epistle 40, CSL vol.III, pt.2; JUR vol.I:556

70

Alphonsus Maria: TRE p.449-453
Hilary: *Cf.* "On the Trinity," Bk.VII, PL 10:202; LOS vol.I, p.61, col.2
Ambrose: "Commentary on St. Luke," ch.4; FOC p.379-380; CSL vol.XXXII, pt.4 (1902); PL 15:1587

71

Vincent: "Commonitoria," no.29, FOC p.354, and no.25, PL 50:637, FOC p.389-390
Tertullian: "Objection Against Heretics," no.15-19; PL 2:12; FOC *cf.* p.366-367; CSL Vienna: 1942
John: SS

72

Cyprian: ANL
Edmund: LFS p.176-177
Epiphanius: "Against Heresies," LXXVII, FOC p.64
Thomas: STL II-II, Q.5, art.3 *ff.*; QUESTIONS AND ANSWERS ON SALVATION, Fr. Michael Muller, CSSR, 1875, Q.32, *From The Housetops*, Still River, MA: 1977, V:5, no.1, Question 32, p.17

73

Leo XIII: "Satis Cognitum," PTC:568, 573
Pius XI: "Mortalium Animos," PTC:854-855 *ff.*
Alphonsus Maria: TRE pp.459-453
Cyprian: ANL

74

Pelagius II: "Quod Ad Dilectionem," DNZ:246; "Dilectionis Vestrae," DNZ:247

75

Leo XIII: "Satis Cognitum," ACTS OF LEO XIII: Supreme Pontiff, Rome: Vatican Press, 1896
V Lateran: SCN
Pius XII: *Cf.* "Orientalis Ecclesiae," ACTA APOSTOLICAE SEDIS, 36:129, Rome: Vatican Press
Pius XI: "Mortalium Animos," PTC:873
I Vatican: *Cf.* "Dogmatic Constitution on the Church of Christ," ch.3, DNZ:1831
John XXIII: "Quotiescumque Nobis," June 29, 1961

76

Boniface VIII: "Unam Sanctam," DNZ:468
Maximilian Mary: MMN p.60
Cyprian: UOC, CSL vol.III, pt.1, p.207 (1868)
Ambrose: "Commentary on Twelve of David's Psalms," XL: 30; JUR vol.II:1261
Patrick: THE WRITINGS OF ST. PATRICK, White, 1954
Pius XII: PTC:1502; "Mystici Corporis," PTC: 1040-1041

77

Leo XIII: "Exima Nos Laetitia," PTC:526
Catechism: COT p.105
Edmund: LFS p.175
Jerome: LAF vol.VII, p.528-529; FOC *cf.* p.286

78

Fulgentius: "On Faith, To Peter," LXXIX, JUR vol.III:2273
Augustine: "On Baptism, Against the Donatists," Bk.IV, no. 24; PL 43:107; CSL vol.LI; FOC p.309, no.1
Fulgentius: *Op. cit.*, JUR vol.III:2269, 2274; PL 65: 671
Augustine: *Op. cit.*, Bk.IV, ch.1, no.1; ch.2, no.2, CSL vol. LI (1908); "Commentary on John," tract VI, no.13, 14; PL 35

79

Athanasius: "Discourse Against the Arians," Bk.II, ch.18, no. 42-43; PG 26

Augustine: "On Baptism," Bk.III:13, 18 and VI:9, 14, JUR vol. III:1625 and 1637

John Paul II: *The Wanderer*, May 14, 1992, p.10, col.4

Catechism: COT p.181

Thomas: STL III, Q.68, art.8

80

Augustine: Sermon VIII, PL 46:838; SS vol.IV, p.254 *ff.*

Leo XIII: "Exima Nos Laetitia," PTC:526

Robert: "On the Sacrament of Baptism," Bk.I, ch.6

Pius IX: "Multis Gravibus.," PTC:229; "Amantiss.," PTC:236

Bonaventure: BRE Bk. VI, ch.5:4

81

Pius XI: "Mortalium Animos," PTC:854-5, 872; DNZ: 2199

82

Cyprian: UOC no's.17, 23

Gregory: *cf.* SS

Cyril: "On Leviticus," XVII:3, Bk.1: "Glaphyr. in Levitic.," FOC p.183

Cyprian: Epistle 75, FOC p.411; PL 4:191; CSL vol.III:2, Vienna: 1871

Irenaeus: "Against Heresies," Bk.III, ch.3:4 and 4:1; PG 7; ANL; Fr. Cornelius O'Leary, SJ, Seattle Univ., p.151-152

83

Thomas: STL II-II, Q.25, art.6

Louis Marie: SOR p.99

Innocent III: PL 217, *cf.* Decr. III, 28:12

84

Clement I: "Ep. to the Corinthians," RCH vol.I, p.249, col.2

Thomas: "Apologye," STM p.169, 214; THE LIFE OF SIR THOMAS MORE, Wm. Roper, Hearn edition of 1716, London: Clay & Sons, Cambridge Univ. Press, 1888
III Constantinople: SCN vol., p.635
Carthage: PL 56:486

85

Margaret: *Cf.* MARTYRS, Attwater, NY: Sheed & Ward, 1965, p.122; *The Marytaithful*, Fr. Fred Nelson, Powers Lake, ND: July-August, 1984, p.59, col.1
Anthony Mary: THE MODERN APOSTLE, Claretian Missionaries, Dominguez Seminary, Compton, CA: 1934, p.28
Thomas Aquinas: STL II-II, Q.11, art.3
Thomas More: *Cf.* "Debellacyon of Salem and Bizance," London: 1533, LIFE AND WRITINGS OF SIR THOMAS MORE, Bridgett, London: 1891
Paul IV: JAMES LAYNEZ, JESUIT, Fr. Joseph Fichter, SJ, St. Louis: B. Herder, 1944, p.179
Leo X: "Exsurge Domino," XXXIII, BULLARUM: Dipolmatum et Privileg., Turin: France & Dalmazzo, 1860, vol.V

86

Ignatius: "Epistle to the Ephesians," ch.16 *ff.*, PG 5:643
Paphnutius: TGC vol.6, p.504
Louis Marie: SOR p.99
Frances Xavier Cabrini: SKL p.155

88

Clement VI: "Super Quibusdam," DNZ:570, b, 1
Leo XIII: "Satis Cognitum," PTC:484
Boniface VIII: "Unam Sanctam," DNZ:469

89

Bede: RCH vol.1, p.273, col.2
Catherine: MCH *cf.* p.374
Thomas: "Epistle Against Bugenhagen," STM p.129
Frances Xavier Cabrini: TRAVELS, Chicago: 1944, p.170
John XXIII: Coronation Homily, PTC:1556
Thomas: "Against the Errors of the Greeks," II:36; PTC:484

90

Thomas: Trial Testimony, STM p.288
Pius IX: "Quanto Conficiamur Moerore," DNZ:1677
I Vatican: "Dogmatic Constitution on the Church of Christ," I, Session IV
Constance: Condemnation of Errors, against Wycliffe: Session VIII, and Hus: Session XV; DNZ:621, 617, 588
Martin V: "Inter Cunctas et in Eminentis," DNZ:646

91

Catherine: SCS p.201-202, *cf.* also p.222
Robert: "De Romano Pontifice," pt.5
Nicholas the Great: DNZ:326; Council of Rome
Pius IX: "Amantissimus," PTC:236

92

Catechism: COT p.286
John Mary: SPIRIT OF THE CURE D'ARS, Bowden, 1864
John: "On the Priesthood," Bk.III, DDP p.60

93

Ignatius: TEXT OF THE SPIRITUAL EXERCISES OF ST. IGNATIUS, 4th rev. ed., London: Burns, Oates & Washbourne, 1923; *Catholic Treasures*, Monrovia, CA: September 1982, no.84, col.1; VOS
Cyprian: "To Pomponius," IV, JUR vol.I:568; "To Pope Cornelius," PGW p.368 CAS p.52; FOC p.34
John XXIII: "Quotiescumque Nobis," June 29, 1961
Cyprian: "Ad Pupianus," LXIX, CSL vol.III, p.732; PTC:455

94

John Mary: THE CURE D'ARS, Msgr. Francis Trochu, London: Burns & Oates, 1955,p.103
Cyprian: "Epistle To All His People," XLIII:5; JUR vol.1: 573; CSL vol.III:2, Vienna: 1871
John XXIII: "Ad Petri Cathedram," RCH vol.III, p.503

Ignatius: "Epistle to the Romans," VII:2, TAF vol.I, p.82; FOC p.124; "Epistle to the Philadelphians," ch.III, II:3; "Epistle to the Trallians," ch's.II & VII; PG 5:643 *ff.*

95

Catechism: COT pp.266, 149
John: *Cf.* "Audi Fili," Schermer, Ratisbon: 1881
Gelasius I: RCH vol.I, p.147

96

Trent: "Prologue," Session VII, DNZ:843a
Bede: Sermon XVI, PL 94:219; SS vol.III, p.273
Trent: "On the Sacraments," Canon 4, DNZ:847
John Mary: SKL p.55
Catechism: COT p.115
Alphonsus Maria: *Cf.* DDP

97

Florence: "Decree for the Armenians," DNZ:696
Leo the Great: Epistle XV:10; PL 54:581
Catechism: COT p.154

98

Thomas: STL III, Q.68, art.1 and Q.72, art.2, ad 4
Trent: "On the Sacrament of Baptism," Canon 5, DNZ:861
Ambrose: "On Abraham," Bk.IV, ch.II:79; JUR vol.II:1324; "On the Sacraments," Bk.I; CSL LXXIII
Zosimus: DNZ:102, n.2; Canon 2, XVI Council of Carthage
Augustine: *Cf.* JUR vol.III:1882
Basil: "On the Holy Spirit," ch.10:26; PG 31; SS vol.III, p.10

99

Bonaventure: BRE pt.3, ch.5, no.2
John: "On Philippians," homily III:4; "On Acts of the Apostles," homily I:8; PG 62:177; PG 51:61; JUR *cf.* vol.II: 1206
Pius XII: "Mediator Dei," PTC:1228
Robert: "On Baptism," Bk.I, ch.4

100

Trent: "On Penance," ch.2; DNZ:895
John: *From the Housetops*, Still River, MA: vol.V, no.1, p.77
Robert: *Cf.* "On Penance," I:13, III:4, TGC vol.VI, p.357

101

Augustine: *Cf.* "Christian Combat," PL40:289
Thomas: SS vol.I, p.293; CA, "Commentary on John," ch.11, Lectio VI:6
Trent: Session VI, Canon 29, DNZ:839; Session XIV, ch.4, DNZ:898; Canon 7, DNZ:917
Clement VI: "Errors of the Armenians," no.15; DNZ:574a

102

Alphonsus Maria: TRE p.216-220
Chalcuth: HOC
Martin V: "Inter Cunctas," DNZ:587
Constance: "Propos. to the Heretics," Question 20, DNZ:670
Leo the Great: Epistle 108, ch.2, PL: 54:1011
Sixtus IV: "Licet Ea," DNZ:725 and 733
Alphonsus Maria: TRE p.224; GGW p.317

103

John: *Cf.* DUTIES OF THE CHRISTIAN, quoting St. Augustine (tract XXVI on the Gospel of John): 1703
Urban IV: *Cf.* "Transiturus De Hoc Mundo."
Nilus: Epistle 39, Bk.III, Allatius, Rome:1668; *cf.* also "Sermo Dogmatic.," ch.5, Fr. Francisco Suarez, SJ, Rome: 1673, p.364; FOC p.349
Denis: WORKING FOR GOD, NY: Christian Press Association, 1912, p.84

104

Leonard: THE HIDDEN TREASURE: The Holy Mass, Rockford, IL: TAN, 1952, p.29-30
John Paul II: LOR June 6, 1983, p.3
Udone: "Collationes," Bk.I:2, ch.28; DDP p.210
John: LFB p.148

Augustine: "Forgiveness and the Just Deserts of Sins, and the Baptism of Infants," Bk.I:24, PL 44; JUR vol.III:1717
Alphonsus Maria: *Cf.* THE

106

Vienne: "De Summa Trinitate et Fide Catolica," DNZ:482
Pius IX: "Singulari Quadem," DNZ:1647
Nicene Creed: *Op. cit.*, DNZ:86
Ambrose: "De Mysteriis," ch.4:20, THE DIVINE OFFICE, revised by decree of II Vatican Council and published by authority of Pope Paul VI, NY: Catholic Book Publishing Co., 1975, p.497; FOC p.173; JUR vol.II:1330

107

Thomas: *Cf.* CA
Augustine: AUGUSTINE THE BISHOP, F. Van Der Meer, London: Sheed & Ward, 1961, p.150, *cf.* note 98; Sermon XVIII:6; JUR vol.III:1496; "Marriage and Concupiscence," PL 44:413; THE SACRAMENTS, Msgr. Jos. Pohle, St. Louis: B. Herder, 1942 vol.III, p.27; "On John," XIII, tract VII; and vol.I, p.247
Gregory: PG 46:417c
John: "The Consolation of Death," II, SS vol.IV, p.363, col.2
Braga: SCN vol.IX p.774
Thomas: STL III, Q.68, art.1, obj.3

108

Gregory: "Oration on the Word made Flesh," PG 46
Eugene IV: "Exultate Deo," DNZ:696
III Valence: DNZ:324
Robert: "On the Sacrament of Baptism," Bk.I, ch.4
Bernard: "Epistle to Hugh of St.Victor," ch.2, no.6
St. Alphonsus Maria: GM p.380
John: LJS p.53
Henry: "Spiritual Discourses," II; THE EXEMPLAR: Life & Writings of Bl. Henry Suso, Heller, trans. Sr. Mary Ann Edward, Dubuque, IA: c.1962
Augustine: "On Nature and Grace," ch.26, no.29, PL 44:261

109

Gregory: "Oration on the Holy Lights," XL:23, PG 36; JUR *cf.* vol.II:1012

Augustine: Sermon CCCXCII:3, FOC p.99

110

Robert: "On the Sacrament of Penance," Bk.II, ch.14

Alphonsus Maria: TRE p.128, no.13

Catechism: COT p.171

John Paul II: "Congress on Penance and Reconciliation," February 10, 1983; LOR March 7, 1983, p.7-8

Innocent III: "Non ut Apponeres," DNZ:412

Basil: PG 31:425, no.b,c

111

Augustine: "Against the Donatists," Sermon XXXVIII; SS vol.2, p.291

Cyprian: "Epistle to Antonius," LII, *cf.* also "Epistle to Cornelius," LVII and "De Oratio. Domin.," PL 4; CSL vol.III, pt. 2; FOC *cf.* p.138; "Epistle to Jubaianus," JUR vol.I:597a; UOC, no.14; LOS vol.III, p.473

Pacian: "Ep. to Sympronian," PL 13:1051; LOS vol.I, p.336

Alphonsus Maria: VOM *cf.* p.37

112

Pelagius II: "Dilectionis Vestrae," DNZ:247

Eugene IV: "Cantata Domino," DNZ:714

Cyprian: UOC, no.14; LOS vol.III, p.473

Zosimus: Canon 3, XVI Carthage, ACTS OF THE COUNCILS: AND EPISTLES, DECRETALS, AND CONSTITUTIONS OF THE SUPR. PONTIFFS, Paris: 1715, vol.I, p.927

113

Trent: "On Justification," Canon 18, DNZ:828

John Mary: THOUGHTS OF THE CURE D'ARS, Rockford, IL: TAN, 1984, p.30

Alphonsus Maria: GMS p.30

114

Augustine: "Nature and Grace," ch.43:50, PL 44:247; "Epistle ad Simp.," Bk.I, Question 2; VOS *cf.* p.102
Trent: "On Justification," DNZ:804
Ephesus: "Catalogue on Grace," ch.8, DNZ:141
Alphonsus Maria: TRE p.113

115

Clement XIII: "In Dominico Agro," PTC:13
Pius XII: Allocution to the Gregorian University, October 17, 1953, PTC:1351

116

Vincent: "Commonitoria," no's.11-12, 20, PL 50:637; FOC p.386-388; JUR *cf.* vol.III:2172
Pius XII: PTC
Pius X: "Errors of the Modernists," *cf.* no.24, DNZ:2024
John Paul II: "Ad Limina" oration to U.S. bishops, October 22, 1983, LOR; *The Wanderer*, December 1, 1983,

117

Padre Pio: PADRE PIO: The Stigmatist, Fr. Charles Carty, Rockford, IL: TAN, 1973, p.104
Vincent: *Cf.* "On the Suppositions of Logians"
Basil: "Moralia," Rule VIII, FOC p.278; PG 31:700
Ignatius: SPIRITUAL EXERCISES, London: Burns, Oates & Washbourne, 1923, p.123-124
Thomas: DDP p.280
John Paul I: *Catholic Standard and Times*, Official Newspaper of the Archdiocese of Philadelphia, Fr. Edward Roszko, OSFS: "Faith Cannot Be Questioned," February 14, 1986

118

Catechism: COT p.15
Anselm: "Proslogion," Bk.I, A CALENDAR OF SAINTS, Vincent Cronin,Westminster, MD: Newman , 1963, p.111
Maximilian Mary: ICS p.xxxiv
Gregory: PG 44

Ambrose: *Cf.* "Commentary on Luke," PL 15:1587
V Lateran: "Apostolici Regiminis," Section VIII, DNZ:738

119

John Paul II: LOR n.49, December 9, 1992
Pius IX: "Ubi Primum," OUR GLORIOUS POPES, Slaves of the Immaculate Heart of Mary, Cambridge, MA: 1955, p.157
Benedict XV: "Ad Beatissimi," PTC:761
Modernist Oath: DNZ:2147

120

Athanasius: *Cf.* "On the Incarnation," PG 26:983
John: THE COLLECTED WORKS OF ST. JOHN OF THE CROSS, rev. ed., Washington: ICS Publications, Institute of Carmelite Studies, 1991
Vincent: "Commonitoria," FOC p.106-107 *ff.*
Leo the Great: "Magno Munere," Epistle 82 to Emperor Marcian, PL 54; FOC pp.113, 356; Sermon LXIII, PL 54:353; SS vol.II, p.150
Sixtus III: "De Jejun.," sermon CXXIX; *cf.* also "Epistle to John of Antioch," VIII:7, FOC p.185-186

121

Thomas: "On the Truth of the Catholic Faith," Q.14, art.12, Garden City, NY: Doubleday, 1955
Pius X: "Sacrorum Antistitum," PTC:738; DNZ:2145
Cyril: *Cf.* Epistle 55, PG 77:292
Pius XII: PTC
Pius XI: "True Religious Unity," PTC:869
Gregory XVI: "Mirari Vos"

122

I Vatican: "Dogmatic Constitution on the Catholic Faith,"ch. 4, DNZ:1800; "On Faith," ch 4, Canon 3, DNZ:1818
Paul VI: LOR
Pius X: "Errors of the Modernists," no.62, DNZ:2062
Pius XI: "Mit Brennender Sorge," PTC:934

123

Pius IX: "Qui Pluribus," PTC:192-193
Vincent: "Commonitoria," PL 50:637
Isaias: "Oration," IV:6, FOC p.62

124

Pius IX: *Cf.* "Qui Pluribus," November 9, 1846
Leo XIII: "Libertas Praestantissimum," June 20, 1888; CODICIS JURIS CANONICI FONTES, 600, Rome: 1923; "Libertas Humana."

125

Gregory XVI: "Mirari Vos," DNZ:1613-1614
Pius VII: "Post Tam Diuturnas," 1814
Pius IX: "Syllabus of Errors," no.15, DNZ:1715
John: LSW p.82

126

Alphonsus Maria: SERMONS, Dublin: Grace, 1845, p.28; *cf.* also PFD p.154
Augustine: Epistle 141:5, CSL 41:238
Robert: *Cf.* "Doctrina Christiana," Paris: 1870
Leo XIII: "Satis Cognitum," PTC:581
Walter: THE STAIRWAY TO PERFECTION, Garden City, NY: Image Books, 1979, p.196

127

Louis Marie: TDM p.190
Francis: LFB p.162
John Paul II: "Reconciliatio et Paenitentia," December 2, 1984, LOR; *The Wanderer*, September 11, 1986, p.2, col.3
Basil: "Longer Rules," XII:2, TGC vol.VI, p.53
Benedict: Rule, VII:21
John Mary: SCA
Augustine: "On John," tract XCVII; SS vol.II, p.341

128

Jerome: *Cf.* "Dialogue Against The Pelagians," PL 23:495
Teresa: SWT p.397-398
Anthony Mary: LIBRARY OF CHRISTIAN AUTHORS, Madrid: 1947
Alphonsus Maria: CAW
John: "Respect due to the Church and Sacred Mysteries," PG 63:623; SS vol.II, p.141
Teresa: SWT p.217; *cf.* also ST. TERESA OF AVILA, William Thomas Walsh, Milwaukee: Bruce, 1943, p.70

129

Maximilian Mary: MMN p.7
Leo X: "Exsurge Domine," Errors of Luther, no.8, DNZ:748
Alphonsus Maria: WPS p.109, no.3
John XXIII: *Cf.* Allocution at St. Paul's, January 25, 1959

130

Vincent: MARY, HELP OF CHRISTIANS, Fr. Bonaventure Hammer, OFM, NY: Benziger Bros., 1909, p.402
Catechism: COT p.410

131

Pius IX: "Quartus Supra," PTC:395
Alexander VII: "Condemnation of Errors," no.5, DNZ: 1105
Pius IX: "Syllabus of Errors," no.17, DNZ:1717
Irenaeus: "Against Heresies," Bk.IV, ch.33:7, JUR vol.I:241

132

John: "On Matthew," homily XXIV, PG 57; SS vol.III, p.91

133

Gregory: "Oration" XVI:15, VOS p.73, JUR vol.II:981
Alphonsus Maria: DDP p.101
Augustine: "On Nature and Grace," ch.36, no.42, PL 44:255, 267; CSL vol.LX (1913)

134

Leo the Great: "Mystery of the Nativity," PL 54:190; SS vol. I, p.118-119

John Paul II: General Audience, September 17, 1986, LOR; *The Wanderer*, October 9, 1986, p.3

Adrian VI: ANALECTA HISTORICA DE HADRIANO VI, Burmann, Utrecht: 1727

John: "Bishops of England, Where are You?" Julia Grimer, *The Angelus*, December, 1985

Gregory the Great: "On Matthew," homily XXXVIII:8, PL 76:1281; SS vol.IV, p.230

135

Clement I: "Epistle to Corinthians," I, ch.39, TAF vol.I, p.67

John: LSW p.337; LJS, p.31

Louis Marie: TDM p.64

Bernadette: SAINT BERNADETTE SOUBIROUS, Msgr. Francis Trochu, NY: Pantheon Books, 1958, p.308

Gregory VII: LFB p.203

Trent: "On Justification," Canon 23, DNZ:833

136

John: THE COLLECTED WORKS OF ST. JOHN OF THE CROSS, rev. ed., Washington: ICS Publications, Institute of Carmelite Studies, 1991

Louis Marie: THE LOVE OF ETERNAL WISDOM, Bayshore, NY: Montfort Publications, 1960, p.133

Robert: LFB, p.19-20

137

Alphonsus Maria: IBI p.292; *cf.* also CAS p.66

John: "To the People of Antioch," homily XL, TGC vol.IV, p.341; *cf.* also GOH p.39

Arsenius: LIFE OF SAINT ARSENIUS, by St. Theodore the Studite

Alphonsus Maria: SERMONS, Dublin: Grace, 1845, p.174

Anselm: *Cf.* SS

Philip: LFS p.132

138

John Mary: GOH p.37
Anna Maria: LIFE OF VEN. ANNA TAIGI, Fr. Callistus of Providence, 5th ed., p.371
John Mary: SCA
John: From the Housetops, Still River, MA: 1977, vol.V, no. 1, p.75, col.2
Thomas: STL *cf.* I, Q.23, art.7, ad 3
Louis Marie: SLM p.144

139

Alphonsus Maria: PFD p.182 *ff.*
Francis: TREATISE ON THE LOVE OF GOD, J. K. Ryan, Rockford, IL: TAN; *cf.* also *From the Housetops*, Cambridge, MA: Fall, 1948, "Liberal Theology and Salvation," Cyril Karam, p.13-14

140

Adrian I: "Epistle to the Bishops of Spain," DNZ:300
Fulgentius: "To Monimus," Bk.I, ch.7:1, JUR vol.III:2254

141

Alphonsus Maria: TRE p.140; *cf.* also PFD
Pelagius I: "Humani Generis," DNZ:228a
Mary: MYSTICAL CITY OF GOD, Ven. Sr. Mary of Jesus of Agreda, Spain, Washington, NY: Ave Maria Inst., 1971

142

Louis: SUMMA OF THE CHRISTIAN LIFE, Ven. Louis of Granada, Madrid: Library of Christian Authors, 1947
III Valence: "On Predestination," Canon 2, DNZ:321
Alphonsus Maria: PFD p.186

143

Augustine: "Corrections," I, 8:6, JUR vol.III:1967; "Enchiridion on Faith, Hope, Charity," XXIII:93, JUR vol.III: 1924
Thomas: CA
Alexander VIII: *Cf.* THE PHILOSOPHIC SIN, Beylard: 1935

Alphonsus Maria: PFD p.166 *ff.*

144

Benedict Joseph: *Cf.* BJL
Alphonsus Maria: PFD p.182 *ff.*
Ignatius: THE CATHOLIC CLASSICS, vol.II Dinesh D'Souza, Huntington, IN: Our Sunday Visitor, 1989, p.100
Gregory the Great: "Moralia," I:15, ch.19, PL 75:509; TGC vol.III, p.120; SER p.162

145

Prosper: "Response to Objections Raised by Calumniators in Gaul," VII, JUR vol.III:2030
Pius X: RCH: *cf.* ACTS OF THE SUPREME PONTIFF PIUS X, Rome: Vatican Press, 1904
Augustine: "Predestination of the Saints," VIII:16, JUR vol. III: 1984
Clement XI: "Errors of Quesnel," no.69, DNZ:1419
Thomas: STL Supplement, Q.99, art.5; art.2, ad 1; *cf.* "Commentary" on Peter Lombard's IVth BOOK OF SENTENCES

146

Alphonsus Maria: WPS p.106-107; *cf.* also PFD
John: "On Corinthians," II, 5:10, homily X; PG 61:471
Thomas: STL II-II, Q.25, art.6, et ad 1

148

Augustine: "Admonit. and Grace," VII:11, JUR vol.III: 1945
Paul III: "Sublimis Deus," RCH vol.I, p.625, col.1
Ambrose: TGC vol.IV, p.335
Caesarius: SERMONS, ed. Germain Morin, PL 39; CORPUS CHRISTIANORUM

149

Pius V: "Errors of Du Bay," no.5, DNZ:1005
Pius X: "Editae Saepe," PTC:729
Gregory XVI: "Summo Jugiter," PTC:158

Augustine: "Against Julian the Pelagian," ch.4:3 and "The Spirit and the Letter, to Marcellinus," ch.27:48, PL 44; "Retractions," II:63 and 88, *cf.* JUR vol.III:1902, 1903, and 1733
Trent: "On Justification," Canon 1, DNZ:811
Paul VI: LOR

150

Wulfran: LOS vol.I, p.385, col.2
Augustine: "Quaestion. Evangel.," Bk.I:3, TGC vol.II, p.92
John: SAINT AMONG THE HURONS, Fr. Francis Xavier Talbot, SJ, Garden City, NY: Image, 1956, pp.271, 78-79

151

Athanasius: *Cf.* "On the Incarnation of the Word," PG 25:95
Eusebius: "Preparation for the Gospel," FOC *cf.* p.215-216; PG 21:21; GCW XL, pt.1, Berlin: 1954; *cf.* also "Comment. on Ps. 17," and "On the Resurrect.," Bk.II; LAF vol.IV, p.496
Maximilian Mary: MMN p.77-78

152

Thomas: "On the Truth of the Catholic Faith," Garden City, NY: Doubleday, 1955, Q.14, art.11, ad 1; *cf.* also ST. THOMAE AQUINATIS: OPERA OMNIA, Fiaccadori, Parma, Italy: 1859, vol.IX, p.246
Pius IX: PTC
Eusebius: "Commentary on Ps. 87," FOC p.271-272; "Commentary on Ps. 86," FOC p.48
Cyprian: "Epistle to Pomponius," no.62, FOC p.52; PL 4; CSL vol.III, pt.2, Vienna: 1871

153

Paul VI: *Cf.* PATHS OF THE CHURCH, Boston: Daughters of St. Paul
Pius XII: RAC:291
Thomas: CA, *cf.* "On the Gospel of Mark"; SS
Augustine: "The Pilgrimmage of This Life," *cf.* SS vol.IV, p. 404, no.2-3; "Against Petilian," no.74, t.2, Epistle 52; FOC p. 199, note 2; PL 43:245; CSL vol.LII (1909)

155

Innocent II: "Errors of Peter Abelard," no.10, "Testante A-postolo," DNZ:377 and 378
Aphonsus Maria: CAS p.xlvi-xlvii

156

Bernard: "Epistle to Hugh of St. Victor, On Baptism," no.77, ch.4, PL 182
Prosper: "Call of All Nations," Bk.II, 17:29, PL 51:647, ANCIENT CHRISTIAN WRITERS, NY: Newman Press, 1952; JUR vol.III:2046 and 2047
John: "On John," homily VIII:1, JUR vol.II:1158

157

Augustine: "Epistle to Sixtus," JUR vol.III:1454; GMS p.252; Sermon LXIX, JUR vol.III:1515; "Against Julian," V:3, JUR vol.III:1907
Thomas: STL I-II, Q.79, art.3 *ff.* and Q.84, art.4, ad 5; II-II, Q.53, art.2, ad 2
Teresa: HMG p.113

158

Alphonsus Maria: IBI
Thomas: STL II-II, Q.10, art.6
Robert: THE SEVEN WORDS SPOKEN BY CHRIST ON THE CROSS, St. Robert Bellarmine, SJ, Westminster, MD: Carroll Press, Thomas Baker, 1933
Frances Xavier Cabrini: TRAVELS OF MOTHER FRANCES XAVIER CABRINI, the Missionary Sisters of the Sacred Heart, Milwaukee: Cuneo Press, 1944

159

Alphonsus Maria: CAS p.159; SER p.371
Pius X: RCH; ACTA PIUS X, Rome: Vatican Press, 1904
Thomas: STL II-II, Q.9, art.7
Teresa: PAD p.33

160

Alphonsus Maria: CAW
Louis Marie: LOVE OF ETERNAL WISDOM, Bay Shore: Montfort Publications, 1960, p.1
Augustine: CA
Louis Marie: *Cf. op. cit.*
Francis: SKL p.139

161

Augustine: *Cf.* "Nature and Grace," PL 44:247
Francis: WORKS OF ST. FRANCIS DE SALES, Dom Mackey, OSB, Annecy: 1892; CATHOLIC CONTROVERSIES, St. Francis de Sales, Rockford, IL: TAN Books

162

Athanasius: "Discourses Against the Arians," ed. Schaff & Wace, NY: 1886
Thomas: STL I-II, Q.89, art.6
Minucius Felix: "Epistle to Octavius," ch.35, PL 3:348

163

John Mary: THE CATECHIST, Very Rev. Fr. G. Howe, 10th ed. London: Burns, Oates & Washbourne, 1936, vol.I, p439
Bernard: "Epistle to Hugh of St. Victor, On Baptism," no.77, ch.4, PL 182

164

Justin: "Dialogue with Trypho," ch.44; JUR *cf.* vol.I:135a
Pius XI: RAC:628

BIBLIOGRAPHICAL CODE

AHM: THE ADMIRABLE HEART OF MARY, St. John Eudes, trans. Targiani & Hauser, NY: Kenedy & Sons, 1948

ANL: THE ANTI-NICENE CHRISTIAN LIBRARY, ed. Roberts & Donaldson, Edinburgh: 1866, Rev. C.Coxe, Buffalo, NY: 1884-1886

AOJ: THE ANGUISH OF THE JEWS, Fr. Edward Flannery, NY: Macmillan Co., 1965

BJL: LIFE OF THE SERVANT OF GOD, BENEDICT JOSEPH LABRE, London: Oratorian Series, 1850

BRE: THE BREVILOQUIUM, St. Bonaventure, Paterson, NJ: St. Anthony Guild Press, 1963

BVM: THE BLESSED VIRGIN MARY, Gregory Alastruey, St. Louis: B. Herder Book Co., 1964

CAS: INSTRUCTIONS ON THE COMMANDMENTS AND SACRAMENTS, St. Alphonsus Maria Liguori, trans. Fr. P. M'Auley, Dublin: G. P. Warren Co., 1846

CA: CATENA AUREA, St. Thomas Aquinas, ed. J. Nicolai, Paris: 1869

CAW: COMPLETE ASCETICAL WORKS, St. Alphonsus Maria Liguori, ed. Fr. Eugene Grimm, CSSR, Brooklyn, NY: Redemptorist Fathers, 1926

COT: CATECHISM OF THE COUNCIL OF TRENT FOR PARISH PRIESTS, trans. Frs. McHugh & Callan, OP, NY: Joseph Wagner, Inc., 1923

CLS: CORPUS SCRIPTORUM ECCLESIASTICORUM LATINORUM (Vienna Corpus), ed. by Vienna Academy of Knowledge, 1866

DDP: DIGNITY AND DUTIES OF THE PRIEST, St. Alphonsus Maria Liguori (CAW vol.XII), 1927

DNZ: ENCHIRIDION SYMBOLORUM, Fr. Henry Denzinger, 30th ed., London: B. Herder Book Co., 1957 (*paragraph numbers cited*)

FOC: THE FAITH OF CATHOLICS, Frs. Joseph Berington & John Kirk, rev. by Fr. James Waterworth, San Marino, CA: Victory Publications, 1985, Keith Gillette, proprietor

GCW: THE GREEK CHRISTIAN WRITERS (Berlin Corpus), Prussian Academy of Knowledge, 1897

GM: THE GLORIES OF MARY, St. Alphonsus Maria Liguori (CAW vol.'s. VII & VIII), 1931

GMS: THE GREAT MEANS OF SALVATION AND PERFECTION, St. Alphonsus Maria Liguori (CAW vol.III), 1927

GOH: GATE OF HEAVEN, Sr. Catherine Clarke, MICM, Boston: Ravengate Press, 1952

HOC: HISTORY OF THE COUNCILS, Bishop Karl Joseph von Hefele, Edinburgh: Clark Company, 1872-1876

HMG: HAIL MARY, FULL OF GRACE, Slaves of the Immaculate Heart of Mary, Still River, MA: 1958

IBI: THE INCARNATION, BIRTH, AND INFANCY OF JESUS CHRIST, St. Alphonsus Maria Liguori (CAW vol.IV), 1927

ICS: IMMACULATE CONCEPTION AND THE HOLY SPIRIT: The Marian Teachings of Father Kolbe, Fr. H. M. Manteau-Bonamy, OP, Kenosha, WI: Prow Books, Franciscan Marytown Press, 1977

IPM: IN PRAISE OF MARY, Fr. Benedict Lenz, CSSR, Chicago: J. S. Paluch, 1945

JUR: THE FAITH OF THE EARLY FATHERS, Fr. William Jurgens, Collegeville, MN: The Liturgical Press, 1979 *(paragraph numbers cited)*

LAF: LIBRARY OF THE ANCIENT FATHERS, Andrew Gallandi, Venice: 1781

LFB: LETTERS FROM THE SAINTS, arranged and selected by a Benedictine of Stanbrook, NY: Hawthorne, 1964

LFS: LETTERS FROM THE SAINTS, Fr. Claude Williamson, London: Wyman & Sons, 1948

LJS: THE LIFE OF JESUS IN CHRISTIAN SOULS, Saint John Eudes, published by Msgr. William Doheny, CSC, 1945

LOR: L'OSSERVATORE ROMANO, Vatican City, Italy

LOS: THE LIVES OF THE FATHERS, MARTYRS, AND OTHER PRINCIPAL SAINTS, Fr. Alban Butler, London: 1759, reprinted by Sarto Books, 1982

LSW: LETTERS AND SHORTER WORKS, St. John Eudes, trans. Ruth Hauser, NY: Kenedy & Sons, 1948

MCL: MARY IN OUR CHRIST-LIFE, Ven. William Joseph Chaminade, ed. Wm. J. Keifer, Milwaukee: Bruce, 1961

MHC: MARY, HELP OF CHRISTIANS, Fr. Bonaventure Hammer, OFM, NY: Benziger Bros., 1909

MMN: MARIA WAS HIS MIDDLE NAME, ed. Jerzey Domanski, Altadena, CA: Benziger Sisters, 1977

PAD: THE PASSION AND DEATH OF JESUS CHRIST, St. Alphonsus Maria Liguori (CAW vol.V), 1954

PFD: PREPARATION FOR DEATH, St. Alphonsus Maria Liguori (CAW vol.I), 1926

PG: PATROLOGIAE CURSUS COMPLETUS: Series Graecae, Fr. J. P. Migne, Paris: 1866 (*volume and column cited*)

PGW: PREACHING OF GOD'S WORD, St. Alphonsus Maria Liguori (CAW vol.XV), NY: Benziger Bros., 1888

PL: PATROLOGIAE CURSUS COMPLETUS: Series Latina, Fr. J. P. Migne, Paris: 1855 (*volume and column cited*)

PTC: PAPAL TEACHINGS: THE CHURCH, selected and arranged by the Benedictine monks of Solesmes, Boston: St. Paul Editions, 1962 (*paragraph numbers cited*)

PTL: PAPAL TEACHINGS: OUR LADY, selected and arranged by the Benedictine monks of Solesmes, Boston: Saint Paul Editions, 1961 (*paragraph numbers cited*)

RAC: THE RACCOLTA: A Manual of Indulgences, Prayers, and Pious Works, by authorization of the Holy See, Boston: Benziger Brothers, 1957 (*prayer numbers cited*)

RCH: READINGS IN CHURCH HISTORY, Fr. Colman Barry, OSB, Westminster, MD: The Newman Press, 1965

RSS: ROME AND THE STUDY OF SCRIPTURE, 4th ed., St. Meinrad, IN: St. Meinrad's Abbey, 1946

SCA: THE SPIRIT OF THE CURE D'ARS: Vianney In His Catechizings, Homilies, And Conversations, Abbe A. Monnin, Paris: Douniol, 1864

SCN: SACRORUM CONCILIORIUM, Archbishop John Mansi, published by Thomas Florentiae: 1759

SCS: SAINT CATHERINE OF SIENA, Johannes Jorgensen, London: Longmans, Green & Co., 1938

SER: ABRIDGED SERMONS FOR ALL SUNDAYS OF THE YEAR, St. Alphonsus Maria Liguori (CAW vol.XVI). 1888

SKL: SAINTS TO KNOW AND LOVE, 1st ed., Slaves of the Immaculate Heart of Mary, Cambridge, MA: 1953

SLM: ST. LOUIS MARIE GRIGNION DE MONTFORT, George Rigault, Port Jefferson, NY: The Montfort Fathers, 1947

SOR: THE SECRET OF THE ROSARY, St. Louis Marie de Montfort, Bay Shore, NY: Montfort Publications, 1967

SS: SUNDAY SERMONS OF THE GREAT FATHERS, trans. and ed. by Fr. M. F. Toal, Chicago: Regnery, 1955

STL: SUMMA THEOLOGICA, St. Thomas Aquinas, First Complete American Edition, Fathers of the English Dominican Province, NY: Benziger Brothers, 1920

STM: SAINT THOMAS MORE, E. E. Reynolds, Garden City, NY: Doubleday & Co., 1957

SWT: SELECTED WRITINGS OF ST. TERESA OF AVILA, Chicago: Franciscan Herald Press, 1950

TAC: TO ANY CHRISTIAN, Letters From The Saints, Benedictines of Stanbrook, London: Burns & Oates, 1964

TAF: THE APOSTOLIC FATHERS, ed. Funk, Bihlmeyer, and Schneemelcher, Tubingen: 1956

TCH: THE CHURCH, Cardinal John Baptist Montini (Pope Paul VI), Dublin: Helicon, Ltd., 1964

TDM: TRUE DEVOTION TO MARY, St. Louis Marie de Montfort, Bay Shore, NY: Montfort Publications, 1960

TGC: THE GREAT COMMENTARY OF CORNELIUS LAPIDE, Catholic Standard Library, trans. Fr. Thomas Mossman, London: John Hodges & Co., 1887-1890

TRE: AN EXPOSITION AND DEFENSE OF ALL THE POINTS OF FAITH DISCUSSED AND DEFINED BY THE SACRED COUNCIL OF TRENT, St. Alphonsus Maria Liguori, Dublin: James Duffy & Co., 1846

UOC: THE UNITY OF THE CATHOLIC CHURCH, St. Cyprian, *cf.* ANL

VOS: THE VOICE OF THE SAINTS, Francis Johnston, London: Burns & Oates, 1965

VOM: VICTORIES OF THE MARTYRS, St. Alphonsus Maria Liguori (CAW vol.), 1954

ONE LAST WORD

You who have gone through this whole work of mine, or even part of it, please pray for me that God may vouchsafe unto me a portion in that holy and exclusive Catholic and Apostolic Church: the *true* Church, the *life-giving* Church, the *saving* Church!

St. Epiphanius
Against All Heresies, no.80, GCW
vol.XXXVII (1933), FOC p.170-171

NOTES

NOTES

NOTES

NOTES

NOTES

NOTES

NOTES

NOTES